The Women's Ministry of
Bethel Memorial A.M.E. Church, San Diego
Presents

A TRIBUTE TO MOTHER
Edited by Cynthia L. Carlisle Fields

iUniverse, Inc.
New York   Bloomington

Bethel Memorial A.M.E. Church Women's Ministry Presents, "A Tribute to Mother"

iUniverse books may be ordered through booksellers or by contacting:

iUniverse
1663 Liberty Drive
Bloomington, IN 47403
www.iuniverse.com
1-800-Authors (1-800-288-4677)

Because of the dynamic nature of the Internet, any Web addresses or links contained in this book may have changed since publication and may no longer be valid. The views expressed in this work are solely those of the author and do not necessarily reflect the views of the publisher, and the publisher hereby disclaims any responsibility for them.

ISBN: 978-1-4401-2148-7 (pbk)
ISBN: 978-1-4401-2147-0 (ebk)

Printed in the United States of America

iUniverse rev. date: 3/5/2009

This book is dedicated to the Mothers in our lives.

ACKNOWLEDGEMENTS

First giving honor to God for without Him there is nothing. I am humbled that God allowed me the gift of the vision for this book. He didn't have to do it but He did and so to Him, I say, "Thank You!" What a mighty and awesome God we serve; a God who loves us unconditionally in spite of all of our faults and shortcomings.

Next I want to express my love and appreciation to the Women's Ministry of Bethel Memorial African Methodist Episcopal Church in San Diego, California. From the moment I joined the ministry in November 2007, you welcomed me with love and open arms and hearts. I have never in my life been so received. When I mentioned the book as a possible fundraiser, everyone saw the vision and grasped it in their spirits and said, "Let's do it!" I cannot tell you what your love and support has done for me. I didn't realize how much I needed to be a part of you but God showed me that I did. I pray that this is just the beginning of many more projects together!

I can't go any further without thanking three awesome women of God who served on my committee for this book, Sherry Thompson, my good friend with her willing, loving spirit and keen eye for detail and always willing to listen and do whatever is necessary to keep me on track; Tedena Wheeler who always has an encouraging word, a woman of integrity and a strong Faith in God. Last but not least Debra Noble. Thank you ladies for all of your prayers and your wonderful spirit of cooperation!

Thank you to Rev. Anthony L. Hughes, Senior Pastor of Bethel Memorial A.M.E. Church for allowing us to run with this project. To the entire Bethel family, thank you for your prayers and support. May God continue to bless and keep you! To all of the wonderful Women, Men and Young People who took part in this project by your submissions, thank you from the bottom of my heart! As I read each submission I am so blessed and encouraged that this is the right thing at the right time. God bless you!

To my best friend and business manager, Sandrea Jackson and everyone at Jackson and Associates, thank you for your support and for being my sounding board. May God continue to bless and keep you! To my little sister, Leah Tooks, much love, keep doing what you do!

Last but certainly not least, I thank my family, Marshall Fields, III, my son, my inspiration and my number one fan; Rev. Dr. Johnie Carlisle, Jr., my loving, caring father; and my brothers Kenneth Carlisle, Craig Carlisle; My sisters-in-love, Doris Carlisle and Cassandra Carlisle and my handsome, wonderful nephews who I love dearly, Brandon, Shane, Caeden, Rhyen, Evan and Jaxen, and everyone else that is a part of my family(whether you like it or not!-ha-ha!) your support sustains me and convinces me that I can do anything! I love all of you beyond words!

INTRODUCTION

"How can I say thanks for the things you have done for me; things so undeserved yet you gave to prove your love for me. The voices of a million angels could not express my gratitude. All that I am and ever hope to be I owe it all to you."

These words are taken from a song written by Andrae Crouch and although he is paying tribute to God, these words are also appropriate when we think of our Mothers. We are the benefactors of their sacrifice, struggle, pain and prayers. We owe them more than we could ever repay and it is because of that debt that this book was written. Birthed from the lives of those who took a moment in time to say, "I love you Mom, thank you, to God be the Glory for the things He has done," this book pays tribute to those Mothers, Grandmothers, and others who stood in the gap as Mothers to raise us to become who and what we've become; It's the least we could do.

As you read perhaps you will see or hear your Mother speaking to you, telling you how much she loves you, that there's nothing too small or too big that she wouldn't do for you. Maybe you will find encouragement and strength to pull you through a difficult time when you are contemplating throwing in the towel. Or it could be that a memory of childhood long tucked away in a dark corner of your mind peaks its head out from hiding to say, "Remember me?"

These tributes are painted with life's brush drenched heavily in deep colors of determination, faith and a deep steadfast belief in God, reminding us of how we got over. Also reminding us that prayer, faith and a refusal to give up was what sustained our Mothers and still sustains Mothers now.

1ˢᵗ verse- My Tribute © 1971 Bud John Songs, Inc. Words and Music by Andrae Crouch

Thank you, Lord for my Mother
For like her there is no other!
Wrapped in her arms with care
Her gift of love, so awesome, so rare.

Thank you, Lord, your light to shine
For picking her out, and making her mine.
Her heart opens wide just for me
Showing with her life what I can be.

Thank you Lord, seems so small
For mere words can't say it all
Her sacrifice, her prayers and tears
Will sustain me till the end of my years.

By Cynthia Carlisle Fields

Rosalind Renee Hill

Dear Mom
By Sonseeahray Thronton

Dear Mom,

When Aunt Sherry emailed me and asked me to write you a letter in your remembrance, I willingly accepted the honor. I began writing and my thoughts were all over the place, I could not focus and I was not sure if I should write a poem or if I should put my emotions on paper, so I decided to testify.

Mom I am so blessed to have had you for my mother. I am a product of you and it is your qualities that shine as a light inside of me today. Mom you were big on gift giving so I would like to share the gifts that you instilled inside of me.

The first gift is the ***"Go-Getter" Gift;*** you see I have seven more courses to complete my Bachelor of Science in Human Resource Management (20 years and I'm still pressing towards the mark). Mom, as far back as I can remember I watched you achieve everything your heart desired. You said I want a home for my children and you bought our first home. You wanted diamonds so you bought diamonds for every finger including mine. You said I want a mink coat, so you purchased a floor length black mink coat, you said I want a Cadillac, so you purchased a Cadillac, and all the while you nurtured three children and gracefully took care of a husband.

The gift of ***Strength,*** you see when you left me; I wasn't quite grown up yet, not to mention that I had to deal with the tragedy of your unexpected death. So I turned to God's grace and mercy and I leaned not to my own understanding, and when I looked into the eyes of your grandchild, my daughter Keierrah, I drew strength the type of strength that helped me to press through the separation of loosing a mother's love, separating from my family, being separated from my own baby girl for three years, separating from my husband which ended in divorce, having major surgery with no one there but my fifteen year old and God, losing a job, house and $2,000 all in one day, loosing a second job. But all the while I kept holding onto God's unchanging hand and I knew that if I held onto the next gift that everything would be alright.

The next gift you gave me was ***Faith;*** trust in the Lord with all thine heart you would say! God has all power! I could remember you relying on him to see you through. Mom, it was this same faith that taught me to love God first and some how in the depths of my soul I knew that everything would be okay. I remember being at Bethel with my grandmother, and my great-grandmother, and then you, oh what a blessing it is to come from a praying family; four generations of women who loved the Lord.

The next gift that you gave me is the gift of **Love.** You see Mom it was your love that taught me how to love and forgive a man who had wronged me and to forgive him, it was your love that taught me that God could make the enemy your foot stool, and the same job that terminated me rehired me with God's increase, it was your love that kept me in the midnight hour when I needed to learn how to love myself, it was your love that taught me how to trust God when I was away from my baby girl for three years, it was your love that allowed me to learn to be free through my spiritual connection to God. It was your love Mom that first taught me how to pray.

The next gift that you gave me is the gift of **Prayer.** Oh Glory to God because the very thing that I learned through your love is God's grace & mercy and how prayer changes things. I learned that if I just give it to the Lord, and learn to allow him to manifest those things that I've prayed for I can do all things through Christ Jesus who strengthens us. Mom it was your prayer and the prayers of my four mothers that have given me Joy, Peace, Salvation, Tranquility, Faith, Balance, Spiritual Awareness, and a hunger for God's word, so that our generations to come can breathe life! I never want our generations to forget where they come from. It is the gift of prayer that has brought me from the world to the goodness of God's purpose for me.

The next gift is the gift of **Peace**. Mom it's not a day that goes by and I don't reflect on your love for me, although some days are more challenging than others, I want you to know that God has given me the Peace to embrace all that I have come through, and I know that he will not put more on me than I can bare. I've seen the mountain top and I've struggled in the valley, but I know that the God I serve has given me rest.

So I say to you that the last gift that you have given me is the gift of **Joy**. Mom this joy that I've found in my resting place, the world didn't give it to me and the world can't take it away, this joy I have is the joy of overcoming adversity, and teaching my child the word of God. This joy I have is an everyday joy an every minute joy, an every second joy, even when I'm in the storm it's the joy that reminds me that I can be joyful about the storm, because it too shall pass!

Mom, I will always love you because you are my greatest inspiration.

Your daughter,
Sonseeahray Thornton

Maternal Gifts
By Sandrea Benyard-Jackson

As a little girl, you combed my hair;
You dressed me and prepared me for the days, weeks and months ahead;
You tended my wounds when I fell off my bike; or scraped my knee as I learned to skate.
You held me close when I cried out at night;
For I was;
Your little girl and you were my protector – you prayed for me.

(Our Father, which art in Heaven.....Hallowed be thy Name.)

One day while no one was looking;
I became a teenager. You controlled my hair;
You made sure that I did not leave the house looking any old way.
You taught me how to tend to my own wounds;
And preached personal responsibility, so that when I fell;
I knew how to get back up.
For I was;
Your daughter and you were still my protector – You prayed for me.

(Forgive us our debts, as we forgive our debtors)

Yesterday you looked up and wondered where those years had gone;
Your little girl was now full grown.
You talked about my hair in all of its iterations;
You sought my counsel on fashion and make-up. It was now my turn to dress you.
You cried with me through all of my trials, tribulations and broken hearts.
Because we were;
Girls, best friends – I prayed for you and you prayed for me.

(And lead us not into temptation, but deliver us from evil)

Today I woke up with you on my mind;
Wanting those moments and days spent together back.
Even in your pain, you helped me move; dried my tears, hauled my things from one city to another.
I sat on your bed and massaged your feet, combed your hair, hummed your song and watched as God called you home.
I am;
Still your little girl, daughter and best friend – You are my mother. Thank you for teaching me how to pray…

(For Thine is the Kingdom and the Power and the Glory, Forever...Amen)

Danny Brown

Granny Goose
By Tonee Addison and Johnaa Battle

*(An Ode to Danny Brown, affectionately known as Granny Goose
on the occasion of her 75th Birthday and presented at a surprise birthday party given by daughter
Marla Howard, son Marvin Brown (Doris), niece Tonee Addison (James), and niece Johnaa Battle
(Carlos)*

Today we celebrate a superlative lady of the hour.
She's bursting with energy and pure soul power.
Christened Danella Irene Quinn by birth
She's the Queen of 739 Santa Isabel Drive-her turf.

Where she reigns supreme over those who enter her sanctuary
Which is high and mighty or just plain ordinary.
She will befriend the homeless as well as the rich
Being a people's person has always been her niche.

Her siblings included Daisy, Sheila, Martina, and Uncle Al
Who's probably watching her from heaven with that Quinn smile!
The youngest daughter of Dr. Alfred Karruthers Quinn
She's known as Danny, Granny Goose, Auntie and friend.

An adjective to describe her would be versatility
In spite of that right foot she's full of agility.
If you don't believe me just watch what looms
If you're disrespectful to adults, she will fly across the room!

Her life has centered around doling out advice
She does not miss church because it is part of her life
She plays that piano that puts others to shame
When she plays, "I Must Tell Jesus" or "How Precious Is Thy Name!"

She's extremely proud of her substantial family
Every time you turn around there's another branch on the tree!
She beget two children, Marvin Corklin and Marla Lynn
Corky was a handful along with his friends.

Corky, Lamont, and Lurch, caused many a scene
Until Auntie emphatically stated, *"Join the marines!"*
Corky inherited your wonderful personality
Now he too is an outstanding citizen of the community.

Marla Lynn inherited your no nonsense demeanor
Tell it like it is or, *"head out the door."*
Corky met Doris and began the extended Quinn tribe
Unto this union Charvette and Marcus arrived.

Then Marcus married Elizabeth and said, *"Let's be fruitful and multiply."*
They begat Marcus, Rebecca, and Samantha
Followed by Alexander and little Brianna.
Meanwhile, Marla was busy with Chris, DaRaya, and Danny.

In the Denver air, Kara arrived without any calamity.
Then Christopher continued the production pace
By the arrival of little Colberts, Jonah and Jace.
The number of great grandchildren now numbers seven.
Who knows there might be even more lurking around the bend.

Aunt there's many tales we could extol about your generosity
Your life has been one big adventure without any pomposity
Whether you ventured on cruises with your friend Peggy
Or partied with your cousins Cecilia, Joanne, and Sammy.

You make scrumptious meals with greens and other fixins'
You're the only one we know who uses detergent to wash her chitlins'!
There's too many praises that reflect your rich life
You are always there to protect and to provide.

The common sense advice that you have imparted to us
Has settled in our brains like rigomortis!
So, we join here today to say, thank you for what you produced.
Thank you for just being the quintessential Granny Goose!

My Heart
By Debra Cross

I wrote this for my girls Arella and Gianina during the time we faced some of our most difficult challenges.

I wake up each day with you on my mind. Joy is the first thing to greet me because the creator has blessed me with you for another day. Fear is next because of the unknown of what today will bring for you. Then hope and sheer will for positivity to be your shroud that today lessons won't be so hard. Frustration because it's not in my power to control; Peace and acceptance in knowing the Creator has a plan for you and I'm blessed to be a part of it. I look in your eyes so like mine as they look back with total trust and it humbles me. I watch you grow opening like a rose; so beautiful each petal opening perfect in its own way. I see you stand tall and strong on what you've learned so far in such a short time; your love and acceptance given honestly, openly, and unconditionally. To see you smile is to see joy at its purest. As we make this journey, I gladly accept the heart ripping pain and profound fear of watching what you may go through. The frustration because I can't control it, but untold joy that I can be there through it with you and that I was given the chance to be a part of something so humbling and wonderful. So daughters of mine, hold on tight to the knowledge that the Creator loves you and has great plans for you and that as long as the Creator allows me, I will be here for you.

My heart is yours, you came from inside my body, came into the world through pain; saved my life with the light and joy you bring. The Creator and you have blessed me when you both chose me to be your vessel into this world at my humblest.

Thank you,

Mommy

Mrs. Arthur Lee Clipper

Our Tribute to Mrs. Arthur Lee Clipper
By Konnie R. Crawford

Personality:
My mother is Strong and Bossy.

Character:
My Grandmother is Spirit-filled, Saint, Wise and Gracious

Attributes:
My Great-Grandmother is Omnipotent, Eternal, and Compassionate; my Backbone, Leader, and Guide. Happy.

Legacy:
My Great-Great Grandmother is Love, Hope, Faith and Generosity.

Margaret Hubbard Knight Powell
August 31, 1916-June 22, 2001

**A Tribute To
Margaret Hubbard Knight Powell
By Vickie Knight Butcher**

Mother Margaret
Mother Africa
Seeker of ancient wisdom
The African Diaspora's diligent, dynamic and obedient child
when Mother Africa cried, *"Where are my children?"*
You answered, *"Here I am!"*
When Mother Africa called her children home,
You gladly went home to the continent…again and again
Taking whosoever would go with you
Nevertheless going and going and going-either with or
without them.

When spirit guided your footsteps to Africa
Whether wearing walking shoes or walking with a cane,
walker or a wheelchair,
Ever optimistic and observant, you were there.
Sankofa Bird
Sankofa Project
Sankofa Life
To go back and remember that which we have forgotten or
Go back and learn that which we never knew.

Ghana, Togo, Benin, Nigeria, Tanzania, Uganda and more
Your dream retirement in Mombassa was not to be.
What you referred to as enlightening the women
The government officials considered as in sighting the women
to unrest and to riot
Your visitor's visa to stay as a welcomed guest in Kenya
was NOT renewed.
An unplanned and spiritual event
to move you on to Trinidad and Tobago's shores
Teacher of the Deaf-many lifelong friendships
Reciprocal gifts.

A cherished friend was Lancelot Lane
A mentor, celebrity, educator and player of the steel pan
You laughed, loved and enjoyed the magnificence of
Maraval and Carnival and Tobago's beautiful Nylon Pools.
Then, back to your deeply dug roots in California and Tennessee
And your final resting place in Bolton, Mississippi.
Ageless, adventurous, active, beautiful and blessed
Wise, witty, gutsy, resilient, capable and extraordinary.

Mother Africa
Mother Margaret
You blessed all of our lives for having known you.

My Grandmother's Legacy
By Beverly Gilliam

This is my tribute to my maternal grandmother, Celia Henderson Dunn. I don't really remember her because she died when I was a very small child, but my grandmother, "Mama Celia" left a very strong and beautiful legacy of womanhood through the generations of her daughters and granddaughters.

What I know about Mama Celia is that she was born on November 17, 1886 in the state of Georgia, one of a family of eleven children. Her family eventually moved to the state of Texas. My grandmother bore 13 children, all of whom were single births, born at home, and lived to adulthood. There were 7 girls and 6 boys. My mother, Mabel, was number 12. They lived in tiny rural towns in Central Texas. There never was much money. Although my grandmother was married, my grandfather chose to be uninvolved until he eventually moved away from the family all together.

Mama Celia was about 5'7" tall and a solid, sturdy built woman. She was what would probably be considered "over weight" in today's culture. But my grandmother was quite proud of her stature, saying that thinner people appeared to be just plain "sickly" looking to her. She fed, clothed and supported her family by taking in laundry. In those days you had to do laundry by hand. It was tedious, labor intensive work. She washed the clothes in a big wash tub with a scrub board. There were two additional tubs to do the rinse and final rinse with "bluing." For the heavily soiled clothes, she built a fire in the yard outside and set a large pot of water and lye soap on top. After wringing the washed clothes by hand, she would then dump them in a big vat full of starch she had boiled in water, wring them out again and hang the laundry outside to dry. After the clothes had dried, my grandmother would iron them and neatly fold them to be picked up by her white customers or their servants. Mama Celia would allow her youngest girls to earn money for themselves by doing the children's laundry.

My Grandmother was an active member of Bethel A.M.E. Church in Hearne, Texas. She served as a Stewardess and in the Women's Missionary Society there. My mother remembers hearing Mama Celia sing and pray as she did her work at home. I also have fond memories of hearing my Mother singing and humming beautiful hymns while she worked around our house.

It is my Grandmother Celia's personality which makes me love her deeply and want to honor this woman I only know from oral stories and the examples of womanhood I observed in my mother and her sisters. My Grandmother's beautiful temperament is reflected in Galatians 5:22-25 which says;

"But the fruit of the Spirit is love, joy, peace, longsuffering, gentleness, goodness, faith, meekness, temperance: against such there is no law. And they that are Christ's have crucified the flesh with the affections and lusts. If we live in the Spirit, let us also walk in the Spirit." **(KJV)**

As they lived out my Grandmother's example; my Mother, Mabel, and her sisters, Ophia, Willie Mae, Catherine, Mattie, Maude and Barbara, all were proud, tenacious women. They took pride in their existence and womanhood, but also; to a greater or lessor extent, each one of them were soft spoken, and gentle yet strong. Lady like gentility and grace has always been the mark of a "Dunn" woman. My Mother and Aunties did their best to instill those same qualities in myself, my sisters and my female cousins as we grew into womanhood. We all knew how much we were loved because our Mothers took the time to tell us and demonstrate how a young lady speaks, dresses and carries herself. You know, a young lady never raises her voice, wears revealing clothes or too much make-up, eats with her mouth open or "pops" her chewing gum. And of course you must always sit with the utmost modesty.

As I stumbled and struggled through adolescence and into adulthood I was very uncomfortable with whom I was. I was reserved, soft spoken, naive, studious, and what I thought to be very un-cool. My friends and co-workers often commented that I was "too nice", "too slow to anger," "too forgiving," "so tactful" and "too subtle." I set about trying to toughen up my image because I thought it was too childlike for a grown woman. Then, I traveled to Houston, Texas with my Mother and her younger sister to attend the funeral of another sister. As I sat on the front row of the church between my mother and two of her sisters, I was touched by the words of the people who rose to speak their last words of respect to my late Aunt's family. They spoke of a woman who was loved by all who knew her, who displayed strength, courage and grace in the face of a painful illness. They spoke of a woman who had a loving and generous spirit, an abiding faith in God; a woman who had been a devoted wife and Mother and wonderful friend to her brothers and sisters.

Within a few years of that funeral, my Mother lost several others of her siblings. The words of their eulogies and expressed memories of others echoed the very same sentiments as before. I came to realize that all of these beautiful and enviable qualities had been passed down by my Grandmother Celia. I realized that this was her legacy; her very special gift to me. I now embrace all of the components of my personality which exemplify my Grandmother, my Mother and are truly reflections of God.

I honor and thank my Grandmother, Mama Celia, who I hope is looking down to see how my rewards here on earth are directly related to her legacy of a spiritually gracious life.

Let your light so shine before men, that they may see your good works, and glorify your Father which is in Heaven. Matthew 5:16 (KJV)

Sherry Thompson

Thank You
By Tara Jennings

I am sending you a very special THANK YOU!!
Today on my 40th year of existence,
I woke up so grateful.

First because of you, I even exist!!
So for that I am most grateful.

Second because of you, I am who I am.
Watching you has made me become the person I am.

You have set a fantastic example of loving and supporting your children.
You gave us your wisdom through experience.

Although you sometimes say, you don't think you prepared us,
I don't think you could have prepared us any more.

Some things are suppose to be experienced on your own.
If my girls take from me half of what I took from you,
I have no doubts that they too will be extraordinary women.

So, even though it is my birthday, I celebrate you!!!
Thank you for giving me life,
and being forever a part of it.

I LOVE YOU SO MUCH!!
Your daughter, Tara Jennings

Harriet Ella Miller
October 8, 1920-August 8, 1981

A Tribute
By Adrian Miller

With a smile that extended from cheek to cheek, and a heart as big as the state of Texas, this Mom knew how to manage, organize and keep everyone of a family of seven encouraged. She listened to and fixed all of her five children's growing pains and problems. Always a mediator through childhood disagreements and helping our father, who was self-employed, get through his ups and downs managing a construction business, was just a few of the duties which confronted her on a daily basis.

She was the Chef, who provided three hot meals each day, and set a table in which all family members sat. A blessing to God for the food was never missing and each person had to say a Bible verse before eating. Manners were emphasized at the table. If you did not obey the rules of, "table manners," you had to get up from the table and eat when everyone else had finished their meal. She could take leftovers and make an unknown dish that could compete with any gourmet cook.

She kept a ledger book in which a page was designated for each bill, each child and miscellaneous items, which included unexpected expenditures. This book was used as a reminder and she shared with each one of us what she bought, when she bought it and how much it cost. We'd watch her total expenditures every month; money brought in and money spent. You could not argue about what she did or did not buy because it was recorded. Her ability to budget was phenomenal.

She was a seamstress who made dresses for three girls, sometimes made out of the same material, using ruffles, binding, or ribbons to distinguish which girl it belonged to. She washed clothes, hung them on a clothes line, starched and iron clothes for seven people. The twin boys were lucky; they got overalls from Sears, and jeans from J.C. Penney's department stores.

She would assign chores appropriate for our ages. We were shown how to do them first and from then on, we were on our own. Chores and school work had to be completed before engaging in any fun activities. This instilled good workmanship and skills which later made each of us employable and accountable.

We were never sent to Church, we were taken by our parents. We all were involved in various activities of the church starting at a very young age. We were challenged at home during the week by being asked Biblical questions so we could be ready for BTU (Baptist Training Union).

Education for us was a priority. Mom was not fortunate enough to have had a formal education, but she taught us to be the best we could be and to strive to achieve. All five of her children have college educations and have worked and are still working on prestigious and rewarding jobs. Mom stressed the importance of having "common sense" and being "God fearing." We often heard her say while working around the house, *"Lord have mercy,"* or *"God bless Your child."* These were just words to us as children, now that we are adults we understand the significance of these words and the impact her wisdom had on each of our lives.

For happiness, joy, sacrifice, and understanding you brought.
For sharing of love, wisdom and being positive you taught
Your legacy of striving to be the best, will linger for generations to come
We can truthfully say you are with God as a special and Chosen one.

We love and appreciate you,
Gladys, Vivian, Dianne, Aaron, and Adrian Miller

What Is A Mother?
By Arella Cross

A Mother is a person who cares for you when you're sick, kisses your owies and makes them better. She knows when you're hurt, knows when you're lying; and always makes sure you're taking your vitamins. She is the beacon of hope in our times of despair, because we know she'll always be there. Not everyone can be a Mother because a woman like…there is no other. This is not a car, or a bouquet of flowers, but, instead, a word from the heart of a granddaughter to her Grandmother. Thank you for all you have and will do.

Love Always,

Arella Cross

Tina Davis-Williams

A Tribute to My Mother
By Helen Martin-Hicks

My Mother, my friend, what can be said about such a phenomenal woman! She ranks up there in the big league. A Mother of nine children who went to college while raising us, she realized her dream as a sewing teacher. She was also a social butterfly. She was recognized by many organizations gaining many awards.

Tina was co-publisher of the Voice News and Viewpoint Newspaper for sixteen years. She also was the creator of San Diego's Ten Best Dressed Fashion Show which recently celebrated twenty years.

Now a resident of Denver, Colorado, she is still as involved as ever. As recent as June 7, 2008, my Mother modeled in a fashion show at her church, Shorter A.M.E. Church.

Mothers are very dear and special. I am honored to be called her daughter.

A Letter to Mama
By Linda Brown

Dear Mama:

I am so glad that I have this time to talk with you. Though you are not physically here with me, you are always here in my heart and mind. Within my soul you are alive today.

The last two days have been cool and as I pulled my blouse sleeve down, because it had bunched up under the sleeve of my coat as I put it on, I felt your work rough hands pull that blouse sleeve down with so much love that I could feel your face close to mine. I could hear you saying, *"Straighten out that sleeve so that you don't look all wrinkled, when you get to school."* As you walked out the door to clean someone else's house, kissing Margret, Ann and I you would remind us to get to school on time. Then when your workday ended you would make sure you stopped by the store and bought the same food for our table as the food served at the table of the people whom you worked for daily. I remember your favorite saying was, *"Whatever I do for those people whose houses I clean, I will do for my family too."*

Mama I always thank you and Poppa for giving us so much; not just material things but life lessons that have stood the test of time and I was the one who needed quite a few life lessons just to make it to that magic age of 21. When I could move out and live on my own or so I thought. There were many false starts to that life on my own and you two were always there with open arms to say welcome back, the rules have not change.

Mom when I was a teenager, I would tell people you and I were so much alike that we couldn't live in the same house and I would say it with anger. I now make this same statement with pride and a smile because with age comes wisdom, that understanding wisdom that has been bestowed upon me by God and You.

As I help my adult children through their life journey, I can only laugh and know you are yet still here and yet still smiling that I-TOLD-YOU-SO smile.

I talk to my grandchildren about their great-grandmother and great-grandfather and all the wisdom that both of you shared with me as I grew up in your light. I use your wisdom with a smile knowing that that is my way of introducing them to you.

Then I smile to myself and say, *"Thank you Sweetie and Teddy for all that you have given me."* You see I want to be sure my children, grandchildren and great-grand children continue to speak your names and therefore your spiritual presence will always be here on earth to protect and guide all of us.

Momma and Dad I love you for being the shoulder that I still stand on as I continue through this journey called life.

Linda

(I know this letter was supposed to be addressed to those who mothered us, but in my mind my father mothered me too. I cannot separate these two spiritual beings who yet still love me, guide me, and are a part of my daily life bread.)

O Lord, you have searched me and you know me.
You know when I sit and when I rise; you perceive my thoughts from afar;
You discern my going out and my lying down; you are familiar with all my ways.
Before a word is on my tongue you know it completely, O Lord.
You hem me in-behind and before; you have laid your hand upon me.
Such knowledge is too wonderful for me, too lofty for me to attain.
Where can I go from your Spirit? Where can I flee from your presence?
If I go up to the heavens, you are there; if I make my bed in the depths, you are there.
Psalm 139:1-8(NIV)

Sassy Sistahs
By Kimberly Coleman
(Dedicated to GG, my beloved Mother and Grandmother to my four Princesses)

Sistahs are Sassy
Yet gentle and kind;
Some humble,
Some bold,
Nevertheless
You will find;
There is an exquisite liveliness
She will lift a somber mood,
Always self-assured
Girlfriend has nothing to prove.
Her character is full of vigor
Even if
Her health is restricted,
Don't hesitate to admonish
If
Her acts of anger seem vindictive.
Usually in control and not vengeful,
She probably warned
Whoever
Not to go there
With her.
Although most always cool
She can rise to a hot temperature.
Her creativity is impertinent

Offering profound new vision,
But handle her heart with care
Or her love for you will go into remission.
This spirit and soul is not to be toyed with
If tested
You may sense impudence.
Caution-this usually happens when a sassy sistah in your presence.
She's yours
Mother, sister, aunt, cousin or friend
Forever standing in camaraderie
A fellow soldierette
From beginning to end.
Never beware though
She loves you-always will
A debonair extraordinaire, any sassy sister's heir
Cannot be concealed.
She is everything good.
A woman is a definite celebration of sistahood!

Remembering Our Mothers
By Bob and Patsy Trice

It is our dear Mothers we remember,
We think of how it must have been for them.
In difficult times our families were raised,
We know not of the troubles they faced.

We remember that our needs were always taken care of.
Tear stained eyes they dabbed softly.
Loving hands fed us,
And with gentle pats we were burped.

Proudly they chose what we wore,
We were always dressed so neat and clean.
And if we fell down and skinned a knee,
A kiss and band aid made it all better.

In silence they must have gone without.
Only when time has stolen our youth,
Do we realize we did not thank them enough?
And now we can not tell either of them face to face.

In our hearts they are our most treasured memory.
We know now, God's greatest creation is – Mothers.
We are thankful for their love,
No tribute is too great for,
Margaret Trice and Otelia Maull.

"Big Mama"
By Sylvia Love

As a child, we would spend the weekend at our Big Mama's house. We would go to church every Sunday with Big Mama because she was on the Mother's Board of church.

She would get up in the morning singing, *"I had a little talk with Jesus and I told Him all about my troubles…"* At that time I would wonder why she sang that song, now I know. In the evening we would sit around her feet and listen to the stories of being raised in the south and then we would do a little Bible study. (No TV back in the day)

The memories of Big Mama are like treasures that you never want to give up.

**Elnora Wooten and
Daughter Ruby Favors**

An Incredible Mom
By Ruby Favors

Elnora Wooten, born May 31, 1925 in Paris, Texas, is a vivaciously attractive woman at 83 years old. Her favorite scripture, "Blessed are those who mourn, for they will be comforted." Matthew 5:4.

For over 60 years, my Mom has been actively involved with the Missionary Society and Head Usher in the church. As children growing up, we could not sleep nor chew gum in church. If we were caught doing either one, we would feel an un-welcomed, heavy thump somewhere on our bodies. She's a strong believer that children should be alert and attentive in God's house.

My Mom is a firm believer in feeding the mind and as a result, all of her children and grandchildren are college graduates. She's also politically active in her community, in Lawton, Okalahoma. She's a long-standing member of the NAACP. Her respect for the community inspired me to walk picket lines and do my part as an active member of the civil rights movement. As a teenage, I was among the first to integrate our junior high and high school in the city.

My Mom is passionate about human rights and feels it is a privilege to vote and leads the charge in driving seniors and disabled citizens to the voting polls. She chaired and served on the board for Neighborhood Watch Committee for several years. At her 80th birthday party, the Superintendent of Schools called her the "Mayor of Lawton View." She is on top of what's happening in her community.

Our house sits on a corner lot where the school bus stops and children play while waiting. One day, a student threw a rock and broke one of our windows. She instantly picked up the phone, called City Hall and insisted that they move the bus stop. With great hesitation and the typical run around you get when dealing with government entities, which was a challenge, the bus stop was moved.

She's a feisty woman that doesn't bite her tongue. She's also a comedian in her own right; she keeps you laughing and is fun to be around. There's no hidden agenda with my Mom; what you see is what you get. She's highly respected, caring and generous. Our childhood house is like Grand Central Station on Sundays with all ages and ethnic backgrounds stopping by to enjoy her company. That's my loving Mom!

Mamie L. Davis

A Tribute to Mamie L. Davis
By Regenia Mack

Affectionately known as Aunt Mamie and "Other" Mom, she is like a mother to us since the home going of our mothers. And we are truly a blessing to each other. She loves the Lord and the Bethel A.M.E. Church family where she serves as a faithful member and in many capacities for many years. Her favorite bible verse is Palms 23.

She also enjoys meeting and engaging in a dialogue with people and a diligent telephone buddy to many friends and family members on a daily basis. We thank the Lord for placing her in our lives.

Love and God Bless,
Regenia and Romeo Mack and the Davis Family

Mothers
By Daesha Hatchett

To my Mommy – I've watched you change & blossom over these last two very challenging years and I admire your strength, courage and endurance. I love you with all I have & all that I am! I *thank you* for all the sacrifices you've made on my behalf. I Love the Nana that you are to my kids & thank God for our sister-like Friendship! I am proud to be your daughter & *thank you* for always being there for me! You mean the World to me!

To the Mother I've shared -"Ms. Ollie Nash" *thank you* so much for your Complete Acceptance! *Thank you* for your unconditional Love & for always keeping it REAL. I appreciate all your support, especially Palm Springs! *Thank you* for including me as your daughter. I Miss you so much! *Thank you* for being my Mom!

To the God Mother of my Children, My Sister in Christ &
"My Very Best Friend" – Tedena Wheeler
When I gave birth to my daughter, you were there. When we celebrated the life of my brother & father, you were there. When I excelled in my career, you were the first to give a toast. When my family was in a crisis,
you were there to lead us in prayer. When my mother had surgery,
you were the first to provide her a homemade meal.
You have always been there for me – through good times and bad.
You have always accepted me, just as I am. I am Grateful that God brought us together. You have taught me many things, more than you know!

I adore your relationship with your daughter & the wonderful Mother you
are, as Aja would say *"She is my Best Friend."*
Something every Mother would love to hear!

I appreciate your marriage and the friendship you share with your husband, I marvel at your sense of style & fashion – Ms. Diva, yes you are!
I respect your LOVE of the Lord - you always place him first & foremost!

Our Family vacations are priceless; our Sunday dinners are delectable,
& our girlfriend conversations are irreplaceable!
I treasure our friendship& I love you most dearly!

Sylvia J. Rogers

To My Mother with Thanks
By Carolyn Rogers-Brown

Thank you Mother for being just a good Mother and friend! I have been through so much over the years and I'm thankful for having you by my side. The laughter and tears have made me stronger, brought me closer to love and understanding, and has improved the way I live. I asked heaven to send me a Mother like you and my prayers were answered. There is nothing on earth more prized than to have you as a Mother and true friend to me.

I love and appreciate you for all that you do.

Your baby daughter,

Carolyn Rogers-Brown

Travis Mae Ward
January 10, 1910-
January 23, 2006

In Honor of My Grandmother
By Sharon M. Davis

My Grandmother, Travis Mae Ward, was born on January 5, 1910 in Waco, Texas. She was a very strong woman who worked very hard for most of her life. She held many different jobs throughout her lifetime, but the most important job that she held was as a full-time Mother. She raised my seven siblings and I after our Mother died in child labor. I was only seven years old. She had no hesitations about stepping up to this task. Not only was she a Mother to me, she mothered three generations of our family at one point or another. From cooking and nursing, to washing clothes in the tub with her knuckles, she was a Mother in the truest form. My Grandmother was a very insightful woman, who knew a lot about life and had many stories to share about her experiences.

There is nothing like having a loving, compassionate Grandmother to care for you when you are sick or hungry. Her food was a blessing to us. She taught me how to cook when I was nine years old. This was one of her greatest gifts to me. To family she was affectionately known as "Grandma" and to church folks she was "Mother Ward."

Grandma was a Christian who loved the Lord. She ran God's race with a smile on her face. On January 23, 2006, Travis Mae Ward went home to be with the Lord.

Motherhood
By Cynthia Carlisle Fields

From your womb I sprang into a world
That could never love me like you.
Your eyes held all the hopes and dreams
That only your mind could conceive.
Perfection looked just like me and
No one could tell you otherwise.

Encouraging me to take my first step
Secretly wiping away the tears that
Had only begun to flow as you knew
That one step would become many.
Learning the hard way the only way
And life would bring me back to you.

Eyes wide open resisting the wisdom
You wanted to share with your firstborn.
Knowing the mistakes I was destined to make.
So patiently you waited and prayed.
"Lord, protect my child." Whispered
daily in God's listening ear.

Now I'm here and you are gone
but not forgotten and my heart aches
Remembering the lessons you feared
I didn't learn yet I carry them in my heart.
Today I am a Mother and those tears, those
lessons and those prayers are mine now
"Lord, protect my child." I whisper
daily in God's listening ear.

Ellen Geraldeen Monroe
March 22, 1916-April 16, 1999

A Tribute to My Mother
By Janice N. Miller

A gentle spirit that was willing to extend a helping hand. Her motto was, *"Open your heart and your doors to others because you never know who will do the same for you or yours someday."* Always accomplishing the tasks she set for herself…finishing high school, receiving her B.A. and going on to complete nursing school.

Her life was riveted with events in her formative years but she never allowed life's challenges to affect her determination. As she shared these events it was never with the intent to frighten or suggest intimidation, but to educate on how you should hold your head up through adversity. Looking towards a better future for her children and those whose path they crossed was her main objective.

Church was such an integral part of our lives growing up that the footprint was established as a family with a firm foundation. Our house was the gathering place for young people, with Mom as the overseer. There were family meetings where my brother and I were allowed to express ourselves with honesty, truth and confidence. My brother always thought he was the favorite but so did I.

As I reflect on the things that made my Mother special, I see the flowers and vegetables my Dad planted yearly. Mom kept vases at the front and back door for freshly cut flowers to be placed, and from the kitchen window she could spot which vegetable was ripe for the picking. She was not fond of the outdoors so Dad brought the outdoors to her, with love. My Mother was an exquisite seamstress…thank goodness because I was smaller than the average girl and had the privilege of having my clothes made especially for me.

During my childhood she was a Great Mom, as a teenager she was a Big Sister and when I married she became my Best Friend. With my sons I have been able to use my Mother's communication skills and wisdom quite effectively and I consider it a blessing and say, thanks Mom.

When it comes to Mothers we all feel ours was/is the best and well we should because it is the truth. I was always reminded by my Mother to be a young lady in all that I said and did and to treat others as I wanted to be treated. As a child I felt this was a reminder, but as an adult I see it was a life lesson to cherish. Cherish, what a beautiful word, it brings tears to my eyes as I think of the true beauty of my Mother.

We miss you Mom…

Eula Mae Johnson

A Tribute to My Mama!
By Akanke Celestin-Ramsey

Unconditional lover of her children, my spiritual mentor, and my cheerleader, that's my Mama!

She has a heart overflowing with love and a spirit of kindness that brings humility to her with ease. That's my Mama!

She is confident and competent when she makes commitments and takes on responsibilities. She is caring and compassionate even when her caring and compassion is not reciprocated. That's my Mama!

My first nurse, chef, manicurist, beautician, counselor, teacher, masseuse, and glam squad, that's my Mama!

At the start of my teenage pilgrimage (1968), my dark brown skin was confirmed as beautiful and worthy of wearing the color red! She set the standard of beauty in our home, which was comprised of multiple skin tones. The standard of beauty in our home was and continues to be, love the skin you are in!

She starts her day with Bible study, intercessory prayers, prayers of gratitude and a talk with her twin sister. She is predictable with her unyielding love for me, committed to excellence, dependable, humble, and loyal to family and friends; a woman of integrity. That's my Mama!

I have learned so many life lessons from my Mama. How to accept the gift of peace that comes from faith in God's words and promises, the power of earnest prayer, the importance of my role as a Christian woman, how to love my husband and children unconditionally and the importance of service to others.

Thank you God for blessing me with Mrs. Eula Mae Johnson as my Mama!

Joyfully submitted,
Akanke Celestin-Ramsey

Deborah H. Gardner

A Tribute to Mother
By Alice E. Davis

My Mother, Deborah, is the youngest of four children. She is the mother of seven children, Grandmother to twelve and Great Grandmother (Granny Granny) to fifteen.

In 1999, my Mom had two knee replacements that were not as successful as we had hoped. The family thought that this would slow her down, but today she uses her two canes to get around. We had to buy her a cell phone just to keep track of her. Deborah can be seen around Oakland driving her van, dropping off or picking up grandchildren; taking her brother to the doctor (deceased February 2008), grocery shopping or picking someone up.

Our house was and still is known as the gathering place where she welcomes everyone and continues to welcome everyone; from the children's friends to now, the grandchildren and great grandchildren's friends. It doesn't matter whether it is a holiday or not, they just stop by. You can always find a meal or something going on at my Mother's.

When there is a celebration, there is always a house full of family and friends; playing cards, dominos or some other type of game-competing to see which team is the winner because we love to compete! Everyone is welcome to eat and celebrate no matter what the occasion may be, even the drop in visitors.

She still gets around in the kitchen to cook her first grandson's favorite meal when he travels home from Atlanta or to whip up her sweet potato pies for the youngest great grandchild. No one is a strange in the Gardner house. There is truly an invisible "Welcome" sign over the door.

My Mother spends the majority of her time with the grandchildren and the great grandchildren teaching, mentoring and sharing her wisdom and knowledge. One of Deborah's hobbies is fishing. Some of our fondest family vacations were of all of us piling into the car and my Mom and Dad teaching us how to fish. This hobby has carried over to the grandchildren.

My Mom has been a source of strength, love, a voice of wisdom; and through the up times and down times, and she has continued to show us the power of prayer and worshipping God. My Mother is the teacher and the hand that has guided our family. The one word that is not in her vocabulary is, "I can't." She will just tell you that you can.

We thank God for blessing us with a Mother as extraordinary as my Mom. She is our example of the Victorious Woman. She has given us values to live by and has showed us what makes her life rewarding by loving her family. I used to say that I didn't want to be like Mom. She has the patience of Job. Now that I am wiser, I pray that I can only do half of what she has done.

On July 21, 2007, my Mother celebrated fifty years of service at Parks Chapel A.M.E. Church in Oakland, California. I pray that God continues to richly bless my Mom and keep her heart encouraged.

I love you Mother…

I praise you because I am fearfully and wonderfully made;
your works are wonderful, I know that full well.
My frame was not hidden from you when I was made in the secret place.
When I was woven together in the depths of the earth,
your eyes saw my unformed body.
All the days ordained for me were written in your book
before one of them came to be.
Psalm 139:14-16 (NIV)

Bertha Williams

Our Mom
By Zoniece Jones

Our Mom-believed that every child could learn. While in her 80's, Mom developed a reading program for children, and applied and received approval as a 501c3 nonprofit organization.

Mom loved her children and grandchildren and her grandchildren's children who could do no wrong! *Our Mom*-would, except on Sundays, prepare breakfast of bacon, sausage, eggs, grits, and maple syrup. On Sundays a special breakfast of rice, biscuits, fried chicken or roast or fried pork chops, Ymm! Ymm! Ymm!!

Our Mom-proud and caring, quick witted, charming, a force to reckon with; determined, proud, demanding, loving and loved, stern, firm, Chiffon dresses, silk blouses, pot roast, gloves classy, sassy, apple turnovers, fried chicken, molasses cake, banana pudding, blackberry cobbler, peach cobbler, lemon meringue pie. Laughter, Kentucky Derby, fishing, grits, scrambled eggs, educated, educator, vibrant, generous, intuitive, homemade biscuits, smothered liver with onions, collard greens, and mustard greens, black eyed peas and ham hocks, sweet potato pie, lemonade, homemade sausages, banana cake, grandkids could do no wrong. One look could stop you in your tracks, and a pinch on the arm is all it took. *Our Mom* was all this. *Our Mom*-special from the top of her head to the bottom of her feet! *Our Mom,* now resting in peace and shouting glory with those who came before!

Love,
Pat, George, Zoneice, Gloria, and Carol

Honoring Our Mother Doris Mae
By Dwana M. Robinson

We thank God for our Mother Doris Mae, because she has reared us in a loving Christian home that we (my brothers Cal and Fred and I) are proud to reflect today.

Our Mother always wears a smile on her beautiful face; she carried it during the post war days while taking a bus/train/bus/bus ride to work after dropping my brother and me at the babysitters before 7am. My brothers and I thought all Mothers smiled until it was brought to our attention that our Mother was the only one smiling in the church choir of 93 members. Her IQ of 145 was rewarded with a scholarship to Howard University in Washington, DC in the early 1940's. However, her parents would not allow their first born to leave New Orleans, Louisiana, to attend school so she continued on life's road with marriage and three children. What a wonderful break for us.

The Lord has blessed our Mother with such grace. She welcomed our friends (6 or 7 extra children) home for dinner after morning church service followed by returning us to church for BTU every Sunday evening. Those friends remember her today with cards and flowers expressing their gratitude for her genuine warmth. Now her family has been extended to include her several health care specialists from Somalia who she welcomes to share after-church dinner with her in Dallas, TX.

Doris Mae is the matriarch of our family; she has, besides her three children, five grandchildren and six great-grandchildren. We thank God every day for all the things He has done especially for keeping our Mother healthy (she wakes up in her right mind - that's our little joke), and showing us that all things are possible…

We love you Mother and will honor you all the days of our lives.

Your Loving Children,

Dwana, Calvin and Fred Fox

From One Mother to Another
In Honor of Eleanor K. Jackson
By Jerald Jackson

Stand strong! The Motherland did,
As her precious metals, jewels and earth
were striped from her head.

Stand strong! The Mothers cried out as their sons and
Daughters were chained and dragged out.

Stand strong! The Mothers shouted out as they looked
while their children were flogged and sold to breed.

Stand strong! The Mothers prayed as the war
For peace got stronger day by day.

Stand strong! My Mother said.
Stand strong, my son and
Don't you be afraid.

Stand strong, son
Because your ancestors said,
"Stand strong!"

Happy 80ᵗʰ Birthday Mom!
From your son, Jerald

Oh Lord, you have done what only you can do
And all glory and honor go to you
Molded me, shaped me after Thy will
Calmed my troubled spirit with a whisper,
"Peace be still."
By Cynthia Carlisle Fields

The Outside In
By Carroll Ann Davenport

It is as though I am living on borrowed time. A time that man had not given or promised my Mother; I would have. Funny, though, when I think back to the time I heard I would not live to see eighteen, I knew then that man had no control over another man's destiny.

Machines, whirring, whining, whistling machines,
Into it old blood flows, out of it comes the clean.
Three times a week I faithfully go,
So that I might live to see another tomorrow.

Sometimes I ask myself, why do I bother.
On bended knees, I call on my Father.
Grant me now the promised blessed peace
Enter me into heaven so that I may be with Thee.

No one knows how much I pray
That God above comes and takes me away
I am the child that my father denies
For I was born of deceit and lies.

I keep telling them that I am so tired,
They keep telling me that all I need is rest.
I keep telling them that I am so tired
Yet they don't seem to understand I've completed
My test.

So now I lay me down to sleep,
I pray the Lord my soul to keep.
When I see your face as I awake
It is Your hands I pray to take.
Grant me peace in your domain
As I wait for the others who remain
Faithfully praising Your Holy name.

Well, it was what it was. No regrets. I lived a simple life. So it was that I died a simple death.

In memory of my one and only Rolanda Cashanne Lewis-July 16, 1923-May 9, 2003

Sylvia J. Love

My Mom...Sylvia J Love
By Marnyce McKell

My Mom, Sylvia Jean (McKell, Johnson, Peavy, Carter) Love, IS the most beautiful woman I know. Her beauty illuminates from the inside to the outside.

At 17, Sylvia was a teen parent (Ms. McKell). She married my dad, Hubert "Nick" Johnson, and had my brother Nicholas Richard Johnson the following year. I had the pleasure of being close to my dad in the final stages of his life. He loved my mom (Mrs. Johnson) very much. I am told by his friends, my aunts and uncles, that when I was a baby he used to carry me with him everywhere he went (even the local happy hours!) Before he passed he told me stories about how he met "Sylvie Jean" and how if it wasn't for my Grandmother...but, that is another story.

As a little girl I loved to watch as Mom would put on her make-up. She would literally draw her eyebrows with the little red eyebrow pencil and outlined her eyes with liquid eye liner with great precision. I could not wait until I could where her clothes. Believe it or not in my teens I did wear her cloths, every chance I could, without getting caught!

In my younger years growing up with mom (Mrs. Peavy) in Chicago, were some great memories, too. We lived in a beautiful flat on the South Side of Chicago in the mid 50's, we went to private schools, and that is when and where I received my shop-a-holic training! Every Saturday, my mom would dress me and my brother up and we would go to the dentist or the doctor, have lunch in a great restaurant where I had a chance to show off all the skills learned in the many glamour and etiquette classes she sent me to. Then we would go shopping. She made me feel like a princess. I picked out all my dresses from the Cinderella, collection, while she set and watched me try on dress after dress; that was the beginning of my designer consciousness, then on to the shoe store. I only wore Capezio's the softest and cutest (and most expensive) styles made for little girls. However, I did not have much choice with my hair; it was Shirley Temple curls, and big bows! Oh yeah! After shopping we would go to a museum or art gallery and that is where she instilled big dreams in us, and told us how we could do great things too, we just had to put our minds to it.

The first prayer my Grandma, Mama Mae, taught my brother and I was, "Now I Lay Me Down to Sleep," but the first prayer my Mother taught us was "The Lords Prayer." She would say the words really slow and we would have to repeat after her. I remember saying (to myself of course), I hope I can remember all these words soon, 'cause I am really sleepy!

We moved to Detroit, Michigan in the mid 60's, I was a teenager. Our house was where all of our friends liked to hang out. During the week we always had rib-eye steaks, crinkled french fries and salad, a meal that my brother and I could cook for ourselves. But come Sunday, Sylvia was cooking dinner and we always had a house full of my Mom's friends.

Now let's talk about Sylvia's friends! My Mom hung out with Aretha Franklin and Aretha's brother Cecil Franklin. We went to the Motown picnics, where I remember watching Stevie Wonder act like a normal kid with vision, wrestling a member of the Miracles. One day David Ruffin gave me a ride to school in his Limo! I had a real crush on Levi Stubbs, the lead singer with the Four Tops, who used to come by quite often too. Will someone tell me why I told my mother that when I got 18 years old I was going after Levi? What did she do? She told him. The man turned into a pure flirt. We were on the guest list for all the Four Top concerts when they were in Detroit from that day on! Needless to say, I did not hook up with Levi Stubbs. I was a shy teenager on the run!

My Mother has always supported me in my creative endeavors, and business adventures. When I was 17 my best girl friends, Leslie & Toni and I got together and started a singing group. I can't remember the name of it to save my life. But, my Mom talked a friend into being our manager. We quickly signed up to sing in the Motown Talent show. He bought us powder blue outfits trimmed in light green and powder blue suede shoes. We sang "Come See about Me," one of the Supremes' hits. Well, we got a reject letter stating that we had no originality (go figure). Some little blind boy who played the heck out of a harmonica won the talent contest that year. They called him Stevie Wonder! Do I need to say more about growing up with my mom? It was a blast.

As a young adult my Mom (Mrs. Carter) was there for me when I made my first great escape to California in the Mid 70's. She was there to keep my son in Michigan for the summers. When I decided to attend college at 31 with my 11 year old son, she thought I had completely lost my mind. But, when I graduated from UC Santa Barbara she was there to see me walk across that stage.

When I started my first business in the late 80's she was on the board of directors for M. S. McKell & Associates, Inc., and made a significant financial investment in my company after Mr. Carter's death. She even moved to Kansas City, Missouri to help me run the business. Although the office assistance was short lived, she never said no when I needed her. In fact she was the firms leading sales person. I would send her to networking events when I was too tired to talk, tell her to bring back five solid leads and she would bring back five-plus and when they called the office they did not want to talk to me! The City of Kansas City Missouri fell in love with Marnyce's Mom. She would coordinate the banquet set-ups for major conferences I coordinated or ran the registration booth, and Mrs. Carter was the hostess with the mostess!

Now that we are in our latter years and we both are senior citizens (what a trip!) she is still the most beautiful woman I know. She dresses to kill, and has plenty of class; she still shops 'till she drops, but mostly dropping catalogs now, and on a good day, she can wear me out in Nordstrom's and Neiman Marcus. Her bark has always been bigger than her bite, but her heart has always been one of love, caring and sharing.

My Mom (Mrs. Love) has been blessed with love, not only the name but with someone who keeps a smile on her face and treats her like the queen she is. How funny is it that God would bring my mother Sylvia Jean (McKell, Johnson, Peavy, Carter) Love through a life of fun and adventure for 73 years and then bless her with "Love" the thing she has given to all she meets in her funny little way. God blessed Sylvia with a husband named "Love" who is giving her all his "Love."

Now I have been given a chance through this publication to present her with words of "Love, Thanks and Blessing" just for being my mom. Thank you Lord, for my Mom; the wind beneath my wings.

Dollie Brown
11/15/23-12/5/04

Our Mother, Our Sister, Our Friend
By Frances Pinckney

My, what a tough lady! What a strong disciplinarian! Did we feel sorry for those trees outside? With ten children being told, *"You're going to get it when you get home,"* or *"I'm putting that one on the shelf for you until later."* Those poor trees never stood a chance at growth. All jokes aside, Mom, you have always been such a joy to us. You gave us so much to be thankful for. You taught us to be the best that we can be, to be kind to one another, to give to those in need, and to respect and love ourselves and others. Your diligence and faith brought about a tremendous blessing and challenge to us. For that, we are truly grateful.

Mom, for so long we have all stood by watching you embrace the many trials of life with such dignity and faith, while never missing a precious or critical moment in our lives. We thank you for always caring, listening, supporting, cheering, and encouraging us. For without your faith in God and tireless prayers on our behalf, there would be no unity. You have now gone to be with our Heavenly Father and we miss you dearly, but it is our prayer that one day we will all be together singing, praising, and rejoicing.

Mom, you put "class" in classy! We love you and will always remember you as:

*D*arling
*O*bedient to God
*L*oving to the family
*L*oyal Christian
*I*ntelligent woman
*E*nchanting

*B*old and *B*eautiful
*R*adiant
*O*utstanding
*W*ise and *W*itty
*N*oble and *N*oteworthy

We love you mom!
Your Children: Delores, Lila, Frances, George, Margie, Phoenicia, Roxcena, Kenneth, Nathaniel and Michelle.

Rosetta Green

Love Made Manifest
By Dr. Ida Greene

These are my observations on who I am, and the factors that contributed to who I am, and my Mother's impact on who I have become.

My Mom only attended school to the third grade because she had to work in the cotton fields in Alabama to help the family survive. She could not read or write and made an "x" where ever her signature was needed. I taught my Mom how to spell and write her name, Rosetta Green. My Mom was so sad and disappointed that she could not go to school, that every day of my life I heard the phrase, *"Get an education, get something in your head; that is something no one can take away from you."* She also would say, *"I wish I could have gotten an education. I would like one of my children to make something of themselves."*

I heard the calling and took up her banner to get an education. I was given the freedom to be in yearly school plays; plays where my Mom came to watch me. I was involved in everything, traveling out of town to sing with the Church choir, at school I joined the Brownies and Girl Scouts and sold cookies; I joined a book club at age twelve, got the family to take out a subscription to Life magazine, which I found out later they could not afford, but wanted to support my desire for learning. We could not get my Mom to go to night school to learn how to read. She worked two jobs; Monday to Friday she worked in a hospital laundry room and on Saturday she cleaned houses for a white lady who was a registered nurse, which my Mom hoped I would become one day and I did. My Mom was so happy when I appeared on television at age fifteen. Everyone sat around at home to watch me and all my relatives in city knew about it even though we did not have a telephone because we could not afford it. I am thankful to my Mom because she allowed me a space to find myself and find my many Mothers. I was emotionally adopted from the age of six by my many other Mothers; my cousin neighbor, Mama Coute;

my sixth grade teacher, Ms Bascom; my neighbor and church member from Hauser Chapel C.M.E. Church of Pensacola Florida, Mrs. Lee; my ninth grade teacher, Mrs. Raglan; and my tenth through twelfth grade teacher, Mrs. Dubose. When I left home to attend nursing school in Chicago, I adopted a Mother at my church, Bethel A.M.E., Ms. Marie McArver, and when I arrived in San Diego at Bethel A.M.E., I was adopted by a church member, Mrs. Veora Conley, plus I had a cousin in Los Angeles, Mama Betty, my only family in California and a cousin in Stroud Oklahoma, who adopted me as her daughter into the Todd family(my grandmother, Adelle Todd Green, who died when my father was age twelve). All of these Mothers helped me to arrive at the place where I am today.

Things my Mom said to me:
"It's a poor dog that does not wag its own tail" (be proud of who you are).
"Always have your own money."
"Never ask anyone for anything unless you have to."
"Mama may have, Papa may have, but God bless the child that's got her own."
"You can catch more flies with honey than you can with vinegar" (be nice to people).
"Don't let your right hand know what your left hand is doing" (keep some things to yourself, especially if it is something new you are starting and you are not sure how it will turn out).

My Mom always had some money tucked away. I never heard my Mom ask my Daddy for money, but I heard my Dad ask my Mom many, many times for money. I realized later that my Mom was the bread winner of the family, but the way she managed it no one ever knew. She made him feel like a man because at that time in Florida black men had to say, "yes sir" and "no ma'am" to all white people. Blacks and whites drank at separate fountains, and we rode at the back of the bus. My Dad was made to feel powerless outside our home. However, he was somebody in our home because of my Mom and we knew it. My Mom vicariously graduated with me when I became a registered nurse. When I got a BS in Psychology, MS in Counseling; when I received my Pupil Personnel Credential to practice as a School Nurse/Counselor; when I received my Lifetime Teaching Credential in Psychology, when I received my degree and license as Marriage, Family, Child Therapist; when I received my PhD in Psychology and when I graduated from ministerial school with a Doctorate of Divinity. She witnessed me writing my first four books which she tried to help me sell to people in Pensacola. My Mom repeatedly said, *"When I was younger I could not get an education, I would like for one of my children to make something out of themselves."* I guess I heard the calling and made her happy. Whenever I went home to Pensacola, Florida to visit, my Mom told the whole city I was coming home and I was treated like a celebrity. It was humbling. The one time when I really knew that my Mom loved me and appreciated me for all I had done for her and our family was when she visited me in San Diego when I was working as a registered nurse. I never polished my white shoes. My Mom polished my shoes everyday; she washed and laid out my work clothes on the bed for me before I went to work on the 3-11 p.m. shift. I am so glad I chose an uneducated woman, who could not read or write, who worked two jobs except on Sundays when she rested to be my Mom. Her thirst for an education allowed her to pass her passion on to me. I love learning and achieving. I will be a continuous learner until the day I die. When my Mom died in 1994 I had written four books, I now have 18 books written. I can see both she and my Dad smiling every time I accomplish or achieve something.

Isabelle
By Yvonne Duncan

My Mother is a pillar of strength
Perfection is the goal she strives for
The perfect person she is not
Human with mistakes and faults

Fears

Emotive

Religious

Silly

Dancer

Always rehearsing her speech
…Isabelle

Thelma Hendricks

A Tribute to Thelma Hendricks
By Frances E. Hatchett

Mama was born and raised in a small town in Oklahoma, the city of Chickasha. She was a God fearing woman; always faithful to the church, St. Paul A.M.E., until her death. She taught us to be faithful to God and do His will.

She worked in the church as a teacher, cook, cleaner; whatever needed to be done and never complained. She had a beautiful voice and sang in the choir. She was a wonderful cook. Our house was on the corner of First and Texas; a good spot for the church ladies to sell dinners, pies and coffee.

My Mom was always helping others. Our door was open to everybody. Our friends hung out at our house because there was always food and she made them feel welcome.

Mama was full of love but she was tough also. She demanded respect; she also gave it. Education was very important to her. She demanded that we keep our grades high. If you didn't there would be no social activities for you. She was active in all of our school programs. She took a kid without a Mother and became his foster Mother and encouraged him to do his best, supported him on the football team and in his grades. She was good at helping others. She also helped to prepare meals for visiting teams.

She was a Gray Lady at the local hospital and also volunteered at the local nursing home. She not only took us to Sunday school and church, she also took our cousins.

Mama was kind, loving, honest and generous. Anything she could do to brighten somebody's day she would do it with a smile.

She is always in my heart.

That's What Flows Through Our Veins
By Cynthia Carlisle Fields

Power and strength to stand and never give up
That's what's running through our veins.
Taking a little and making a lot because survival was not a choice.

Trained on how to sit with our legs crossed, hands in our laps
Respecting our elders and keeping our opinions to ourselves
While our minds were free to think and dream.

Like a river our blood intertwined feeding our hands, our feet
Yes, that's what's running through our veins.
Courage to walk a path twisted, turning and unsure
Marching forward with our hand in the invisible hand of God.

Our eyes, hearts and ears focused on the lessons
Passed down from Mother to Mother, daughter to daughter
Like precious gold we keep them close, protected in our spirits
Trespassers will be shot for treading on our Holy ground!

These temples of grace and beauty polished by His Presence
And so we smile because we know that God's grace is sufficient
And that is what flows through our veins!

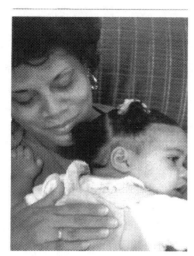

Marla Howard

The Gift of Life
By Dannella Howard

Usually, when mothers experience the blessing of bringing life into this world, they are overflowing with emotion and excitement. I was born July 31, 1989. There was no emotion flowing from the woman who was once my mother. I'm sure she was excited, but not because she gave birth to a healthy baby girl. She was excited because my birth brought her one step closer to being discharged from Yakima Memorial Hospital, and one step closer to her next fix. She was one step closer to being freed of her parental rights, not only to me, but to my older sister DaRaya. She was one step closer to succumbing to the climaxed life of a drug addict. But where did this day bring me? I had no future, no bearing. I was nothing more than an existence. My sister and I yearned for the love and warm embrace that only a mother could give, but our biological mother was unable to give us. That's when Marla Lynn Howard stepped in and embraced us. Her arms were like the wings of an angel sent specifically to us by God. Marla Howard gave us life.

My Mother has done the unthinkable by taking on the responsibility that another woman chose to leave behind. Many adopted children feel resentment towards their biological parents for giving them away, but I don't. If I had the opportunity to say anything to my biological Mother, I would simply say, thank you. I would thank her for the decision she made because she gave me the chance to have a Mother that is deserving of the title; a Mother who would give me adequate care and attention that I need. There is no other woman in this world I would want for a Mother except Marla Howard.

My Mother has instilled the importance of faith and a personal relationship with God within me and my siblings.

"With God, all things are possible, trust and believe in Him, and there is nothing you can't do." She would continuously remind us.

She has proven these words to be true. My Mother is my role model because she has been the primary caretaker for me and my siblings for the past ten years. Somehow, she finds a way to provide us with our every need, without ever showing a sign of weariness or wanting to give up. She is the epitome of strength and confidence. My Mother has taught me that there is a distinct difference between existing and living. There are many people who wander this world with no expectation, or sense of direction. Sure, they have the ability to function, but that's it. They simply exist. My Mother has given me the opportunity to live. She has taught me morals and values, and guided me with faith throughout my life thus far. She has helped me to set my goals as high as the sky by showing me that I can be anything I want to be with hard work and determination.

Mom, I feel the need to express my love and gratitude for you. I can say that I have made it this far because of you. You've done so much for my siblings and me, putting us before yourself on numerous occasions. I don't know where I would be if it weren't for your kind, devoted heart. I sit back and think about my life and the things I have, such as: family, friends, cats, belief, contentment, serenity, ethics, and self-respect. I know I have these things because of you. It is because of you that I not only exist, but I live. Each day when I rise, you are the first person I think of. When I lay my head to rest, you are my final thought before I sleep. It's good for a Mother to feel loved and treasured by her children. I love you more than I love myself. I entered this world lonely, but knowing that I have God by my side, and my Mother in my heart, I am never alone.

Your daughter,
Dannella Irene Howard

Akanke Celestin-Ramsey

Dear Mama
By Jacquelyn Alisha Celestin

D-Don't you know that you are my best support? My dance teacher, my boxing coach, my life coach?

E-Every time we talk I learn something new to tuck away in my mental list of things to tell my child one day.

A-Always in style! My Mother is sophisticated, classy, a showstopper! She walks into a room and all heads turn!

R-Remember when I wanted to dance, be a gymnast, an artist? I remember you taking me to every class, cheering at every performance, my biggest cheerleader.

M-Magnificent laugh! My Mom and I share the same sense of humor and share giggles that only we understand.

A- A nurse practitioner, women seek her expertise and kind words. She gives her patients a dose of Mother's love that brings them comfort.

M-Making a difference; active in the community, with every person she meets, my Mom leaves an indelible mark on their lives, just like she has mine.

A-Are you aware of how wonderful you are? What a blessing it has been to be your daughter? My dear Mama…

Love,
Jacquelyn Alisha

Nana
By Aja Wheeler

It seems as though you are just on one of your voyages….maybe on a cruise or in Turkey marveling at the beautiful sites. But, in reality, you are gone.

I never thought that I would have to experience the emptiness I feel because you are not here with me. I'm sad because I can't hear your angelic voice call me "Dolly Dimple" or feel your warm embrace as you give me those special hugs that I adore so much. But sadness is not what you want from me, so I'm happy that you have finally made it. You have made it to that place called Heaven; the land flowing with milk and honey.

Nana, I just want to say that I love you. I love you more than anybody knows. When it's my turn to finally settle down and have kids of my own, I will boast of my Grandmother, my Nana, my angel just as you boasted of me to your neighbors and friends. No matter what Nana, I will always think of you and all you've done not only for me but for our family. I couldn't possibly write all that is in my heart, so I ask God to forward all that's in my heart to you so that you will know and feel how much you will ALWAYS mean to me. I love you Nana, always and forever.

Xoxo,

Aja

HONEY
By Christine Peterson

Being one of seventeen children I was told that you were the only one with a nickname. I asked why, but there was no real answer, perhaps you were favored, perhaps you were unique, perhaps the color of your skin, perhaps your parents knew that the taste and the scent of honey was good and hard to resist. Perhaps they knew 'Honey' had been around a long time and was soothing, healing and helped to strengthen.

Your father, Jacob, was an Assistant Pastor at Campbell Chapel Methodist Church. Being in church was something that was required coming up as a child. This rearing has certainly set a foundation for you and allowed you to have an awesome relationship with God, and because of the rearing and the relationship with God, He has increased your life in many areas.

Honey, (Vivian Patterson), my Mom, one of the older seventeen, was the first to have a grandchild (me – Christine). You delivered me at home with a midwife, no hospital. You worked at an early age and very hard while I stayed at home with my grandmother and played with my younger aunts and uncles.

Mom, I remember you telling me the story that one day (between 3 – 5 yrs) I was riding in the back seat of my grandfather's car and fell out, onto the road, from playing with the door. I was scarred all over my body. You and grandmother nursed me back to health using butter and old remedies to heal my wounds. *I must say your love and the soothing hands from "Honey," I was healed and made whole, and I don't ever remember having scars. I LOVE YOU MOM!*

Mom, I remember you used to work cleaning houses and I would go with you sometimes and we used to take baths together because at my grandparent's house we did not have a bathroom, out houses and silver tubs was what we were used to. *Bathing with you was a very special time for me and I will always remember the bonding. I LOVE YOU MOM!*

Mom, I remember when you stepped out on your own and got our first apartment, a one bedroom place. You, Patrick and I shared the same bed. Your husband was out to sea for the short time we stayed there. *Finally out on your own, a young woman putting a roof over our heads, caring and loving for me/us along with the responsibility of being the sole provider and paying bills. I LOVE YOU MOM!*

Mom, I remember that I had a tremendously high fever and was lying on the couch in that one bedroom apartment and my uncles were standing over me and you were asking me if I could recognize any of them. I did, however, I got the names mixed up and you cried hysterically and quickly took me to the hospital for fear that I was going into convulsions or something. You were quick to respond to my need. *That was the first time I ever remember seeing you cry on my behalf, and though I was sick, I felt your love. I LOVE YOU MOM!*

Mom, I remember when we first came to sunny California in 1967. I knew that you were so excited and happy to leave Virginia. This was something that none of the other siblings would dare to do, leave Virginia and to top it off, *catch a plane – WOW!* God had heard your prayers. You were adventurous and determined enough that this California was going to be your new home and you would not give up the opportunity to better your life. After all a plumbed bathroom, no more cleaning other people's houses, no more picking potatoes and no more working as a cook. As the song says you were "Moving on Up!" *I think the biggest motivator for staying in California was Patrick and I; a place you felt had many opportunities. You put me/us first with every decision made. I LOVE YOU MOM!*

Mom, I know you don't remember this because you never knew, but when you were not at home, working long hours to support Patrick and I, when I needed to feel your presence I would go and lay at the foot of your bed. Every now and then I would fall peacefully sleep because of the comfort I felt. I would get up straighten the bed as if I were never there. *That satisfied my emotional needs. I LOVE YOU MOM!*

Mom, I remember when I moved out at 18, because of course, "I was grown," but not sure of how I was going to completely pay the bills. When I worked with the youth programs during the summer I had to give you half of my check because I wasn't saving it like you told me. I thought that was the meanest, cruelest thing you could do to me – *TAKE MY MONEY THAT I HAD WORKED FOR!* Well when I moved out the nicest, greatest thing happened, you had saved the money for me and gave it to me. I was very surprised because I thought you had spent it. Not only did I have money, but I was allowed to take my bedroom set and other things that I didn't even pay for. *I'll never forget how overjoyed I was and how loved I felt along with how sorry I was for thinking such mean thoughts. I LOVE YOU MOM!*

Mom, I remember during my marriage how you tried to help me to consider my decisions concerning my husband and Tomisha. Though it seemed like I was not receptive and quite defensive, I heard you and considered your advice and there were times I would look back and realize that you were right. You never stopped voicing your opinion – even unto this day, whether or not you feel it is being received. You know that it is your place as our Mother, Matriarch of the family and being obedient to God, to continue to express your thoughts to guide us and make us consider our decisions. The older I get the more I listen and the more I pass down your wisdom to my daughter. *Even when you threw your hands up and said, "Oh well," you took it back and stood by our side. Thank You. I LOVE YOU MOM!*

Mom, I remember having Tomisha, and you came to Long Beach and stayed with me to help with Tomisha. When Tomisha's belly button fell off I was nervous and too scared to even look at it. I asked, "Mom where is it, is she going to be okay?" You could see the fear that was all over me as a new Mother and assured me everything was alright. *It's nothing like your Mom being there with you at such a significant time, and I was truly blessed to have you there, helping me and bonding with your new grandchild. I LOVE YOU MOM!*

Mom, I remember when I called you crying because I was told that I had the BIG "C" – cancer. You stopped what you were doing, drove over and we held each other and wailed and wailed. Out of all the birthday presents I had given you this one was the worst, but it also was the best because from then on our bond got stronger. You sat with me through all my long chemo treatments and you made sure that I had everything I needed when I was at home. You researched and you asked others opinions about my well being, I felt like a kid all over again, because I knew that you would "kiss it and make it feel better." *You were wonderful and so supportive. I LOVE YOU MOM!*

Mom, this is just a taste of the wonderful things that you have done for me. But most of all you've given me/us the same foundation that your father gave you – God. You have on many occasions laid flat on your face and cried out to our God on my behalf. You have fasted for me, prayed for me and spoke one on one with God about me and for me. You've received the peace and strength needed from Him in the rough times so that you may continue to bless me/us with kind words and support. God has granted you much grace and mercy to continue to be the Matriarch of this family. You have been both Mother and father, (and now grandparents), to me/us and I'm sure that this is not an easy job. From the bottom of my heart I appreciate all that you have done, doing and will do. I thank God for selecting you to be my Mother. *I LOVE YOU MOM!*

God is all knowing, and it is evident because he gave my grandparents - your parents (Jacob & Bessie) the insight to call you Honey. They knew that you would be a scent I could never forget, enjoy the taste of a Mother's kiss, skin that's smooth and rich, can't resist no matter how I tried, soothing to the touch with healing power, but most of all strong enough to keep this family together no matter what came our way. I pray for you all the time as you pray for me. I thank God for such a wonderful gift of "Honey."

'HONEY' YOU ARE THE BEST; OH, DID I TELL YOU – I LOVE YOU MOM!

Life's Gift
By Michaelle Helene Page-Gray

Life is an intricate melody with a twist of unexpected denotations and inflections
It is the beat of a heart, the drum of a tune only heard through the soul
An amazing feeling of relief with a slight strain that is only released through the chords that
holds it together.

Passion is necessary
Love is vital
Success is refreshing
Drive is imperative.

The road that it leads to is forever changing and full of surprise
The hope that it brings lights the world
It is the world.

As sweet as a baby's cry
As tender as the touch of a rose
As gentle as a kiss
As special as it is because it belongs to you.

It is the reflection of everything ever known before me
It is the image of everything before you
A true gift is within the one who created you
The one who you gave life
It is a treasure buried deep, hidden and wrapped tightly
The birthing place for unseen victory, prosperity, abundance and everlasting faith.

Because I believe, in Him is Life's Gift.

A Mother's Tribute
By Dominic Gunder

Donald, Dominic, Norman, Anita, Dexter, Cheryl, Daniel, Daryl. Rita Gunder gave birth to eight (8), yes, 8 children. Count 'em. She was always in baby diapers, and baby bottles and crying babies, and babies tugging at her skirts. After hers eventually came grandchildren and then great-grandchildren – in addition to nieces, nephews, and theirs after them. I never knew when Momma wasn't blowing noses, or bandaging scrapped knees, or brewing some 'ol folks' remedy.

One day, Daniel split his big toe in half while cutting the lawn with the lawnmower. She just stitched it up the best she could and ran him off to the hospital. That boy, she even birthed him at home right on the living room sofa. Cheryl was delivered in the car on the way to the hospital. Anita had this big navel, which had to be cut down to size. Dominic always asked, *"But why?"* and Momma said I cried the first 9 months of my life! Norman was always in trouble at school and brought home bad grades and black eyes. Dexter was the cute one with his curly hair. Donald, the oldest, was Grandma <u>and</u> Big-Momma's favorite. Daryl was the baby and could never do no wrong.

Momma worked full time as a LVN nurse at Mt. Sinai Hospital on Miami Beach. And she had to cook and clean for her husband, Donald. They have been married now for 55 years! Made sure his food was on the table - if we kids left any for him!

Forgot the most important thing – she went to church every Sunday. Made sure we all got up, fixed Sunday breakfast (grits, eggs, bacon, and toast/biscuits) and marched us off to church. Momma sang in the choir (Rev. Kelly told her, 'well if you can't sing soprano or tenor and you can't alto, just sing also'). Later, Momma became a Stewardess and many years later under the urging of Rev. Mitchell and the Holy Spirit, Momma was eventually ordained a Local Elder in the African Methodist Episcopal Church.

When I was in college, I started sending Mother's Day flowers to my mother. She said her favorite flower was the carnation and not roses. Years later, I figured out she didn't want me spending the extra money on roses. Years after that, I realized the flowers didn't matter; she just appreciated the love I sent her way. I didn't miss one year until last year and this year. You see, I was never home for Mother's Day for over 30 years. I was away in college, then the Navy and subsequently settled in California. Last year and this year I didn't have to send my love, I was there in person! From here on out I want to be with Momma to celebrate with her.

I forgot the holidays! Christmas, Thanksgiving, Easter, Memorial Day, July 4, Labor Day, birthdays. There were plenty of days for the family to get together and everyone wanted to come over to our house. Cousins, aunts, uncles, friends and well if you showed up you had better grab a plate because there were no guests in her house. Everybody was family.

I love red roses and violets blue
I love sweet cakes and blueberries too
But more than flowers and sweet things it's true
More than anything Momma, I love you.

Akanke Ramsey and Alexus Ramsey

My Mama
By Alexus Ramsey

A- is for **Amazing** advice

K- is for **Kind** to everyone even during her strife

A- is for very **Attractive** style like the Egyptian queens who used to hang out by the Nile.

N- is for **Nevertheless** the best Mother in the world!

K- means that she is the **Kindling** to the growing fire of my hopes and accomplishments.

E- is for the **Encouraging** words she always gives me.

As you all can see this is how good my Mama is to me.

I love you Mama!

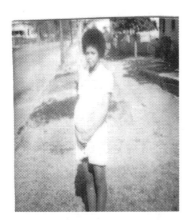 

Mom aka Woo
By Kyelunye Lewis

Most **O**utstanding **M**ember of our family who is always **W**inning **O**thers **O**ver! Through out my life you have provided me with values, rules and expectations. You always told me I could conquer the world and that there is nothing different between me and Donald Trump! You are my biggest cheerleader and my best friend. To put you into words would be, sassy, energetic, persistent, determined, loving, understanding, beautiful hats, wonderful dresser, chef, great mother, wonderful grandmother, spiritual, advisor, protective and caring.

As a child I never understood why you were protective and swore I would never be like you as a parent. Now that I am a parent I realize what you had to endure and how wonderful of a parent you are and I am proud to say I too parent the same way. You did a great job and I hope to do the same. I celebrate you **MOM** aka **WOO** and I thank God for You.

Love,
Kyelunye
Andrew and Fredrick

My Tribute to My Mother
Mabel Gilliam
By Deborah Babe Evans

The passing of my Dad, Brazil Gilliam, has shined a new light of discovery for me regarding my Mother, Mabel. I have enjoyed more one on one time with her more than ever before. Memories of Mommy, Mama, Mom, Mother, have come flooding back to me. Beverly, Artice, Judith and myself, all know w hat a kind, warmhearted, serious, open thinking, Mother we have.

Her strength is mind blowing and her spiritual confidence has held our family together in times of trouble and grief reversed it into unity, pride and acceptance.

I love to sit and talk with her for long enjoyable interludes, because Mom's humor and attention to special details, keep me in the loop with our tight knit family that she and Dad created. When I am troubled, I can call on her to help me see all sides of a difficult situation and she is the first one I call with unexpected triumphs.

I have been a SGI-USA Buddhist for 35 years and as a true Christian, my Mother is one of the strongest spiritual guides I have ever studied.

I have chosen this picture because it shows the lengths my Mother's love extends to. Just recovering from a serious health scare and still visiting my Dad daily, she and my dear sister Beverly, took time out of their lives to ride the train for three hours to Los Angeles to attend Mom's youngest grandson's (my son Sage Evans) High School graduation ceremony in 2007. She said, *"I have attended all my grandchildren's graduations and I would not miss this one for the world."*

My Mother was called "Sweetie" by all 12 of her sisters and brothers (now all deceased) and if you know Mabel Lee Dunn Gilliam, I know you agree.

I pray everyday of my life for my Mother's excellent health, longevity and unsurpassed happiness and I am proud to include our Mother Mabel in the Women's Ministry's, "A Tribute to Mother," because she is not only the Mother of my family, but to our extended family, the community and all who need her warm shoulder to rest on.

Ethel Mae Chance

Ethel Mae Chance
By Wyoline Morton and Rickey Jayne Viganati

She was a loving wife, loyal friend, wonderful Mother, and a devoted member of Bethel A.M.E. Church for more than 50 years. We miss you every day.

With love and the utmost devotion, Wyoline Jayne Morton, Rickey Jayne Vignati and Sonia and Michael Morton and great grandchildren, Ashley Marie and Rickey Michelle Morton.

Piccola L. Harrison
1899-1990

Remembering Mother
By Julia Cooper

The first book of Psalms epitomizes my mother.
The word "Psalm" in Hebrew means, "Book of Praises."

Blessed is she that walketh not in the counsel of the ungodly.
This was my Mother.

For she delighted in the law of the Lord.
This was my Mother.

She was like a tree planted by the rivers of water,
whose leaves remained green
bearing plenteous "good fruit." Her offspring are
prosperous. Currently, at least
ten of her descendents are regular worshippers at
Bethel Memorial African Methodist
Episcopal Church.

She was wife, mother, sister, grandmother and friend.
A true humanitarian who
Served the Lord with gladness to the end!

Hallelujah! The race is run!
Eternal life is gained
My happiness is just begun,
The Crown of life obtained.

Piccola L. Harrison
1899-1990
This was my mother.

Minnie Eberhardt Cobbins

Reminiscing Through the Decades
Memoir of Cobbins Family Reunions
Submitted By Zenola Maxie(on behalf of the Cobbins Family)

We take a few minutes to reflect back during these decades as to our beginning to the present.

In the year 1955, Mrs. Minnie Eberhardt Cobbins was due to visit her children in Chicago and Michigan City, Indiana. She suggested to them and the daughters in California the idea of having a family reunion during her visit here that year. The idea was accepted by the family and plans were formulated for the reunion which was held in July 1955 at Memorial Park in Michigan City, Indiana. Mrs. Cobbins was surrounded that year by her sisters and brother, all of her nine children, all of her grandchildren, many cousins and friends. Zenola and Eddie Maxie were living in Michigan City at the time and were responsible for a great deal of the festivities of the day. It was indeed a grand day and our mother and grandmother, Mrs. Cobbins was granted one of her dearest wishes when all of her family gathered together on that beautiful day in July, 1955.

Several years passed without another official reunion, except the gatherings of the Cobbins children and some of the grandchildren with their mother in Chicago and in California. In 1970, some years after the passing of their mother, the Cobbins family decided to have a family reunion. This was held in Kingsport, Tennessee hosted by Alfonzo and Inez Ervin. There was such a warm and gratifying feeling from this gathering that the sisters and brothers decided to continue with the reunions; to be held every two years. We went from one day to one weekend.

In 1972, the reunion was held in San Diego, California at the home of Johnnie and Joseph Owens. Other hosts and hostesses were Lurean and William (Bill) Taylor, Ann and Searcy (Mickey) Pilkington and Zenola and Eddie Maxie. We continued our festivities in Los Angeles in the homes of Thomas Edwards and the Odell Walkers. The reunion grew larger this year with many cousins and friends joining us and some relatives meeting for the first time. During our visit, a busload of us went to Las Vegas.

Because she was appearing in her own show on Broadway, Micki Grant did not arrive in time for the San Diego festivities but joined us in Los Angeles. By a fortunate coincidence, another production of, "Don't Bother Me, I Can't Cope," was opening during our stay and some forty or more family members attended the preview or opening night performances. The show's director, Vinnette Carroll, joined us on our day with the Edwards.

In 1974, plans were set for Chicago with the reunion being held the last Saturday in July at the home of the Perkins and Murphy's. Other hosts and hostesses were the James Cobbins', the Lucius Bolton's, The John Smith's and Mary Maxey. We were entertained in the homes of each. Over 100 relatives and friends attended the reunion and the activities continued with an overnight visit to Michigan City, Indiana, with Mrs. Hattie Gray serving as hostess, from there on to Michigan where we spent a beautiful day on the lake and in the home of our cousin, Mrs. Annie Hodges and her family. During the reunion, while making plans for the next two years, Inez Ervin suggested the family go on a cruise together and we met in the home of Tillman Polk to discuss the same.

In 1976, plans for a cruise to the Caribbean were put in motion with Tillman Polk as tour leader. There were about 69 persons who enjoyed, some for the first time, a most beautiful Caribbean cruise stopping at five ports. We shall all remember that beautiful trip on the Boheme Ship. We must say, the only mar in the reunion was the absence of the one Cobbins son, James and his wife, Elizabeth, who were unable to attend because of her illness. Ports visited: San Juan, Dominican Republic, St. Thomas, Haiti, and the Virgin Islands.

In 1978, we returned to San Diego, California. The reunion was held again in the lovely gardens of the Owens. We were entertained beautifully and graciously by all of the family members and dear friends of the family, including the Curtis Moring's and Attorney and Mrs. Charles Fielding in their lovely homes. A day was spent in Los Angeles and the usual trip to Las Vegas for three days. We were very happy that year to have some first cousins, the children of Lucius Eberhardt, to attend this reunion for the first time. We agreed that year to extend the reunion name from Cobbins Family Reunion to the Cobbins, Eberhardt, Goolsby Family Reunion.

It is now 1980 and we're together again by the Grace of God; back to Memorial Park, were the first reunion was held. We your hosts and hostesses from Chicago and Michigan City and Micki Grant, from New York, are grateful for the opportunity to host again. We're getting older now and can't take as much, so activities for this year are reduced to five days. Let us remember for a few moments all of our dear relatives and friends who started out with us and joined us through the years, but the good Lord has seen fit to take them from us physically. Their memories shall always be cherished and be present with us.

Memorial List

Mrs. Minnie Eberhardt Cobbins	Mrs. Jacqueline Howell
Mrs. Mattie Eberhardt Jennings	Mr. Robert Lewis

Mrs. Laura Eberhardt Taylor
Mrs. Mattie Eberhardt
Mr. Lucius Eberhardt
Mrs. Anna Ware
Mr. Osar Perkins
Mr. James Gray
Mr. Alonzo Ervin

Mr. Louis Saxon
Mr. William Cobbins
Mrs. Elizabeth Cobbins
Mrs. Susie Griffin
Mr. Robert Eberhardt
Janice Tyson
Kenneth Ervin

In 1982, we journeyed south to Kingsport, Tennessee. We were graciously entertained by Alonzo and Inez Ervin. We always remember that Fish Fry that lasted most of the night. On Sunday we enjoyed a lovely banquet-dinner at the beautiful estate of Nora Alexander. We also enjoyed a trip to Knoxville, Tennessee to the World's Fair and a tour of the Eastman Kodak Company. The finale of the reunion was at the lovely home of Mary Lyons.

In 1984-*Go West Young Man, Go West Young Man!*
1984 found us in the beautiful city of Los Angeles, California with Mattie and Thomas Edwards as our hosts. The agenda for that year was very interesting. Headquarters was at the Amfac Hotel. We took a trip to the "City of Lights," Las Vegas, Nevada and enjoyed the gala celebration of Thomas and Mattie's 50th wedding anniversary. We took a trip to San Diego where we were graciously entertained by Bill and Lurean Taylor and Eddie and Zenola Maxie.

1986 took us the Windy City of Chicago, Illinois. The Perkins and Murphy's were our gracious hosts. Headquarters were at the McCommick Hotel. While there we had five days of fun. We had a wonderful tour of the city and a shopping spree in a suburb of Chicago. The finale was held at the lovely garden home of the Murphy's.

1988 found us in the sunny hot state of Arizona. We journeyed to Mesa where James and Dorthea Cobbins were the gracious hosts. The reunion headquarters was held at the fabulous hotel, The Pointe, in Phoenix, Arizona. We had a wonderful time while there, everything was held at The Pointe. The picnic was on the picnic grounds called the "The Rooster." The family banquet was also held at the hotel. The hotel furnished a full course buffet breakfast each morning and Happy Hour from 4pm-6pm. The finale was held at the home of James and Dorthea Cobbins.

In 1990, because of Gussie's illness, we returned to Chicago, Illinois and again the Perkins and Murphy's were our hosts. The headquarters were at the Quality Inn near the Loop. We were graciously entertained with many festivities including a night out at Oprah's restaurant. The finale was held at the lovely home of the Murphy's.

It is now 1992 and family reunion is being held in "America's Most Beautiful City," San Diego, California, hosted by Bill and Lurean Taylor and Eddie and Zenola Maxie. As in years past a wonderful time was had by all.

Beatrice Bryant

Mama
By Charlene Norwood

Colorful, sparkling bangles and beads
Matching your glistening eyes and your
Radiant smile.

Lightly stepping with a sway in your walk,
Confident and assure.
Carmel skin that has been gently kissed by the sun.

Gracious,
Elegant,
Lovely little lady.

Poised with a strong opinion
And a generous laugh.
Huge package in a tiny body.
God fearing, friendly, lovable,
Mama that's you.

I thank God for you,
For your support, guidance, endless love and
Your sparkle.
I love you

Bernice Wimmes

My Mother-Bernice Wimmes
By Jo Ann W. Vance

Believes in God
Everlasting life is promised to her
Raised her family in the church
Never doubting, always hopeful
Innovative, intelligent praying woman
Comforts the needy
Encourages her family to trust God

Wonderfully and fearfully made
Inner peace is what she seeks from God daily
Mother of Glenn, Jo Ann, Darroyl, Cheryl and Crystal
Mighty woman of God
Embraces her husband and family with love
Special elect lady of God, Bernice Wimmes, my mother!

l-r; Shelia Watts, Sandra Arnell, Harryette Morris, Sonja Reid, Othelia McDonald

Glenna Reynolds

Remembering Mother
Dedicated to Glenna Reynolds by her five daughters

Daughter #1
Sandra Arnell

When I was growing up, those were the best days because I was sharing them with Mama; and I remember feeling safe in Mama's embrace. When we had the air raids during World War II, she made me feel as though everything was going to be okay and nothing would happen to me as long as she was around. Mama always made the good times great times and the not so good times so much better!

I remember Mama seeing that we had the things we needed. She comforted us, making each of us feel as though we were the Special One! Mama prayed that she would live to see all five of her daughters graduate from high school. She taught us how to pray, be honest, respectful and to have high morals.

Christmas was especially special with favorite decorations, food, music and family traditions. Mama made so many wonderful things about the season even more magical. She showed my sisters and me what the spirit of Christmas was really about through giving, caring and sharing. Being close to Mama on that happiest of holidays meant so much to me. Her memory still lives on and I always think of her but much more at Christmas.

Daughter #2
Sonja Reid

My family was made up of five girls, a set of twins of which I was one and three singles. I remember Mama telling us each of us had 1/5 of her love and it would always be there for us at all times. Each day Mama showed us that love and special time. Her life revolved around her girls; making sure we would be prepared to one day care for our own family.

Church, family, school and community involvement was important. With her zest for life and fun she introduced us to many activities; swimming lessons, library trips, visiting museums, the park and playground. She taught us social graces, how to be polite and kind to everyone as we were all God's children.

A strong believer in prayer and that God would always take care of us; there is so much I remember and hold in my heart, her courage, patience, gentleness; being not only my Mother but a trusted friend and letting me know how loved I was.

Daughter #3
Othelia McDonald

It's raining, and we can't go outside. It's such a gray day; there's nothing to do (no television in those days). Mama would say, *let's go see the silver dancing fairies!"* We would run to the windows nudging each other so we could see. There were five of us-all girls. So Mama would tell the eldest girl to hold up baby sister so she could see. We looked and looked and sure enough when the rain fell hard on the black top, large drops of silver seemed to be dancing. *"There they are,"* she said. *"Do you see them dancing?" "Yes!"* we responded. *"I see them, I see them too,"* we all agreed. And today, whenever there is a hard rain, I look for the silver fairies dancing. That is how I know Mama is always with us turning a gray day to silver!

Daughter #4
Shelia Watts

I will go all the way back to early school days; thinking of how Mom would walk to our school to bring us boots and umbrellas on a rainy or snowy day. The care and concern she gave us-never ending. She gave birth to five girls (twins and three singles) but everyone thought she had a set of triplets and twins. We were close in age and looked a lot alike.

Mom and I would catch the bus to go downtown to shop at Lexington Market in Baltimore, Maryland just to get fresh potato chips, pickles and special kosher hot dogs to take to the movies near by. What fun we enjoyed spending that time together. She made time for each of us to do special things with. With five girls there was always something to shop for; prom gowns, dresses, shoes, makeup, etc. to make our days or events so special. She showed each of us how to cook and serve for special occasions, plan parties, writing cards and let us all know how to grow up and become mature adults and prepared us for life to come.

The love she showed and gave of herself was endless. Church was a must. Swimming lessons, family and togetherness was a very big part of her life. It's hard to give just a glimpse of the life of someone very special who gave so much to my sisters and I.

Daughter #5
Harryette Morris

As I sit and think about the love for Mama, I think about the patience she had and how hard she worked without complaining to make sure our basic needs were met and how she encouraged us to grow and to hold our heads up high and to be proud of our family. She taught us to always look after and appreciate each other no matter what. We were her family. I watched Mama love life; she laughed and enjoyed herself and was involved in everything we did. She would listen with an open mind but rarely made decisions. She shared her love and talents with all.

I am the woman I am today because she took time to teach me life's lessons by example and action in a Christian way; they never went unnoticed or unexplained.

Dear Ann Landers
By Robyn Broughton

(This letter was written to Ann Landers in February 1978, when the author was 16 years old in response to a letter that appeared in Ann Landers' column. Robyn is the daughter of Audrey Taborn)

Dear Ann Landers:

I'm a 16-year-old female in a one-parent home. I just want to comment on the letter from "Florida Mom" who complained that as her children got older they became more irresponsible and disobedient.

I took her little quiz, asking kids how much we do for our parents, and I can say I answered most all the questions positively.

I'm writing because I want to know if "Florida Mom" ever bought a bag of chocolates or a toy home for no reason at all. Or, instead of using the "talk it out" approach only when the kids needed discipline, did they have the time to talk when the kids had worried looks on their faces or when they felt good about something? Were Mom and Dad ever honestly interested in their feelings?

Well, my Mom doesn't do much cooking and sometimes she isn't too insistent that the dishes be washed right away. She's brought lunch money and notebooks to school when I've forgotten them, and then been late to work. She's always been interested in what I've had to say. And as I get older I realize that one reason we get along so well is that she's always been around when I needed her.

"Florida Mom" mentioned that she and Dad really love each other, but I didn't find anything in her letter about loving the kids.

If I had to choose my Mom all over again, there's no question as to who I'd pick, and she knows it.

California Kid…and Lucky!

In May 2007, Celiene was honored at the annual "50 Best Moms" luncheon after her teacher submitted her essay to Time Warner Cable who sponsored the countywide essay contest. Approximately 2500 essays were submitted. Celiene was among the 50 essay contest winners.

The Best Mom
By L. Celiene Holeman-Age 10

The New World Dictionary describes Mother as, the qualities characteristic of Mother, as maternal and affectionate. New World Dictionary also describes great as, important, highly significant, and distinguished. Hands down, my Mother is incomparable.

MOTHER
M= Magnificent
O= Outstanding
T= Terrific
H= Happy
E= Excellent
R= Remarkable

My Mom is special because she spends time with me. It means a lot to me because she makes time to spend with me even though she is very busy. My Mother works hard to provide me with a good education. She also helps the community by donating her time to help those less fortunate than we are.

My Mom is unique from other moms. She enjoys taking our family camping. She is very talented. My Mom sews, quilts, and crochets. Sometimes she makes her own jewelry. My Mom is handier than my Dad around the house. She fixes the motor home, she changes the faucets, and in our old house, she even installed the rain gutters and put in a new bathroom sink.

My Mom wants me to have good social skills. She takes me to etiquette classes. My Mom gives me different experiences. She takes Karate, Girl Scouts, horse back riding lessons, sewing and knitting classes. My Mom has taught me to be friendly and to speak up.

I love my Mom because she buys me clothes when I need them and I love to go shopping with her. I love my Mom most of all because she cares for me, loves me, hugs me, feeds me, and takes me to church.

Mom (English); Madea (slang); Mama (Spanish); Maman (French); Mamman (Italian); Mama (Russian); Amma, Oma, Orammi (Asian). Regardless of the language spoken, Mom still means love, still means someone to care for you, help you, and kiss you when you're feeling sad. Mom still means love!

My Mother
By Audrey Taborn*

This photo of my beloved mother won a prize in the San Diego Historical Society's "Faces of 2000 Family Photo Contest" and was on display at the Natural History Museum in Balboa Park.

The photo was taken in 1914 and is a photo of the nurses of Hubbard Hospital in Nashville, Tennessee. My mother, Frances Boyd is directly behind the woman in the front and to the left. Frances graduated from the nursing program at Meharry Medical College and then went on to earn a second degree in education from Fisk University in Nashville. Se taught high school for a while in Cairo, Illinois. In 1925 she married Raymond Dow Taborn and settled in Cleveland, where she worked as a private-duty nurse while raising three children. Later she worked as a registered nurse at Women's Hospital where she won the Ideal Nurse Award from the Cleveland Press in 1948.

Audrey Taborn passed away on Sunday, July 20, 2008.

Lillie Beatrice Greene-Maxwell
1908-2002

A Tribute
Lillie Beatrice Greene-Maxwell
By Mavis Maxwell-Young

Lillie B. was an awesome Christian role model. She loved life and all that God gave her. She never forgot to thank Him for everything. Anyone who knew her knew her Christian values. She loved the Lord and her church dearly. She was a saintly woman who was well respected.

My Mother was hard worker and she taught her four children good work ethics and values. I now garner much strength from the fruitful life she lived. She went home to live with God in 2002. Below is some of the quotes of wisdom she frequently used. She used many more, however, space and time will not allow me to share them all.

<u>Lillie's Quotes of Wisdom</u>

"Everybody's got to mind somebody."
"A hard head makes a soft behind."
"Takes one to know one."
"Taught sense is better than bought sense."
"Say what you mean and mean what you say."
"It's better to be married than burned."
"If you sleep with dogs, you'll catch fleas."
"Practice makes perfect."

Her favorite thing to say was, *"I really enjoyed it."*—that meant food, travel, new experiences, church, family activities, etc.

Daisy Pauline McFarlin

A Tribute to My Mother
By Antoinette Tooks

Mama
Daisy Pauline

Nurturing, demanding
Wife, sister, aunt, Grandma Mac
Mentor

Daisy
Loved to garden
Cooking, sewing, cleaning,
To take care of her family
Pauline

**Our Mom
By Randi Watts**

I know that everyone thinks there Mother is the crème de la crème. But truly ours is. I will try to make this short and sweet because I could go on forever.

Funny thing is my sisters and I were sitting, having a conversation and sharing lots of laughs earlier this evening; remembering all the good times we had growing up-the values, morals my Mother instilled in us at a very early age. She took the time to cultivate individual relationships with each of us; knowing that each of us was different and had different needs. She instilled a sense of pride in each of us that gave us the confidence to face the world with healthy self-esteem. There was never any doubt that we were well loved. We laughed about how wherever we lived, we lived like tourists; trips to the museums, beaches, parks, libraries…there was nothing in any city we lived in or visited that we were not going to experience. She taught us to respect and appreciate the diversity in others and to be open to experience all that life has to offer.

Our Mother is an amazing woman who gives endlessly of herself. She raised her three children and now plays a VERY ACTIVE part in the lives of her six grandchildren.

With Our Endless Love and Appreciation,

Randi, Charlyn, and Sonia

A Tribute
By Rev. Anthony L. Hughes

Mother Gwendolyn Hughes is loyal, dedicated, kind, friendly and generous to everyone she meets. Her smile lights up the room. I am so thankful for my Mom's guidance throughout childhood. I would not be what I am today if it was not for Gwendolyn Hughes, a dedicated woman of God who gives from her heart. She has the gift of giving and loving those whom she meets.

I am so thankful to God for my Mother's wisdom and outstanding example of dedication and giving.

My Gift from God
By Judith Gilliam-Downes

My Mother is my gift from God. She grew up with the nickname Sweetie, and boy can I tell you why. My Mom is the matriarch of the Dunn and Gilliam families. My Mom's name is Mabel lee (Dunn) Gilliam, the 12th of 13 children. She was born October 28, 1928, in Hern, Texas. My Mom is the only living child left from her Mother, Celia Dunn.

The Gilliam family suffered a great loss of our father, my Mom's husband Brazil Gilliam on November 6, 2007. Growing up my Mom taught us to have a love for God as she has. My Mom has always had a strong and faithful relationship with God. She has been able to deal with what most would call unbearable, but she just keeps going on. My Mom says she has been able to do it all only by prayer and the grace of God. Through her love for God she has taught us to always trust and lean on God in times of trouble.

I want to thank her for her love, understanding, and patience in dealing with my family and me. I hope to someday be at least half the person that my Mom is. I thank God every day for my gift, my Mom.

Love,
Judy

I Remember
By Tedena Wheeler

"Train a child in the way she should go and when she is grown she will not depart from it."

And, train she did! My Mother was the granddaughter of a minister and that probably had something to do with our foundation. My earliest memories are of church. One of the very earliest of falling asleep on her lap with my head resting on a bulletin! And then there were the "circle meetings." The precursor to today's Prayer Meetings. Yes, where my Mother went so did her children. And of course, Vacation Bible School, Sunday school, Catechism and participation in the annual Easter and Christmas programs were mandatory. Needless to say, our speeches/recitations HAD to be memorized and properly enunciated.

I remember the Sunday afternoon services throughout the San Francisco Bay Area. I remember the reverence for "Sunday."-No work on Sundays, except for us washing the dishes. I never understood why washing the dishes didn't get the benefit of the "no work on Sunday's" clause.

I remember that our church family was indeed our family. We all grew up together. We all spent time together; in and out of church. To this day, my dearest friends are the result of being involved in Church.

I remember calling my Mother for scriptures pertinent to the theme of an Anniversary, Annual Day or other event that I was chairing. I remember after she relocated to San Diego, we became even closer and she actually dubbed me her "prayer partner." I remember us spending Mother's Day together feeding the Rachel Women's Center.

I remember that it never really mattered to my Mother what Charles and I were doing as long as Aja was with her! Aja and I often have our moments and she recently remarked how "Nana" made all of her "grands" feel special. We all know that we gained our very own Angel the day that God took you from labor to reward.

And, although this is truly only a snippet of my remembrances of my Mother; it's at this point, the easiest to write about. Partly because I also remember that I am a witness to God faithfully rewarding those who serve him and keep his commandments. I remember the scriptures you had each of us read to you during those last weeks. I remember your desire to go home and sleep in your own bed. I remember your last walk to your front door. I remember how all of us held vigil, 24/7 eating only at Charles' insistence to "keep up our strength." I remember that Charles' culinary skills accelerated to a new level as that was his "therapy." And, yes God remembered your faithfulness and took you home to Glory.

I remember that God answers prayers.

Dena

Ella Mae Tooks

In Tribute to
Ella Mae Tooks
By Lawrence Tooks

Loved God,
Her husband (L.E.) and two sons-Lloyd and Lawrence.
Adored her grandchildren-Leah and Lyle.

A loving heart extended to many
Always cheered for the underdog.

Worked diligently and faithfully in the church.

Grateful to Aunt Essie and Uncle Coleman Portlock.

Full of laughter and fun
A blessing to others.

A Tribute
By Rev. Dorisalene Hughes

Mother Doris Franklin sacrificed all that she had for children all over the City of Kansas City. Mother Doris was an awesome asset to the Foster Grandparent Program in Kansas City. She was featured in the Kansas City Star newspaper and awarded a plaque for the Esther Award for the outstanding Grandparent of the Year on June 12, 1998. Doris Franklin gave and continues to give her all as a Mother to all children. She worked in the field helping young Mothers care for their children. She often sacrificed personal safety to help young single Mothers living in depressed and dangerous areas of the City. God has blessed me with such a shining example of God's love for others through service and sacrifice.

I can truly say I am grateful to God for the example she has set for young Mothers and their children!

Myrtle Heath

What My Momma Said
By Felicia Nash

Never be known as a liar or thief.

Treat yourself well. It sets the standard for how others treat you.

Cross me once, shame on you; cross me twice, you're a bad mother (shut your mouth).

It don't take all night.

Why dream of marrying a doctor when you can be a doctor?

You're not in love, you're insane.

What you don't know makes up a whole new world.

Not only have I been around the block a few times, I'm a marathon runner.

Momma knows…

Droops: An Ode to my Mother
By Jasmine Silver-Ferebee

Oh, how many times had it really slipped my mind?

As the strongest root that I had embedded growing up,
You provided foundation and strength for my everything.
Mamma Bear to her cub, you and I always joined—
Be it in the support that you laid or the all that you selflessly gave to me.
Nevertheless, the point is that we were somehow indivisibly linked so that I am in you,
And ultimately you in I.

Yes. Yes, Mom, You did bring me into this world.

Such a funny thing it is—this you and I being eternally linked.
I vowed daily throughout each of my pubescent years
To never, ever become anything like you.
You wanted safety, moderation and feat for my future.
I wanted fun, excess and thrill in my present.
You see, you were like a storm in the evening of my June day.
I just couldn't understand you.
Sadly, you understood me well enough to know that my route
Was rather perpendicular to Success road.

And Yes. You could take me out it you wished.

It is trite reflecting back on me: The umpteenth child in history to lovingly
Embrace the saga of the young and dumb.
Through it all, however, you never abandoned your cub and you owned that role
As Mamma Bear to me.
Rather it was out of love, duty or simply you had nothing better else to do, you were there.
You never have left.
I choose to believe that is the deed of Love.

You always said You could have taken me out of this world if you so chose.

Hustling to provide, fighting the world for life so that I could just make it.
Make it enough to succeed and personify that vision you saw when you first brought
Me into this world.
A vision I never had privilege to see, yet I know I represent your dreams, your aspirations, your
blood and your tears.
As an embodiment of the fight in you, I stand now proud of our link.
A link that not only grounds my feet, but buttresses my spine.
Your doing, my benefit, our link.

But you never did. And for that I do insist my thanks.

Such a funny thing it is—this you and I being eternally joined.
Spirit to Spirit. Woman to Woman. Mother to daughter.
How your strength runs through my veins and sustains me.
How your wisdom guides me through daily.
Oh, how did I not understand you?
Overjoyed to now understand you.
You wanted only the best, and you obtained that the only way—
better yet the best anyone could know how.
Thank-you, Mamma Bear.
Thank-you, my protector.
Thank-you, Mom.

My Tribute
By Donald Ray Hatchett

I believe my Mother has the biggest heart. My Mother loves to cook and is always willing to provide a meal as well as the comfort of her home to family as well as friends. My Mother is loved by so many people that she is referred to as "Momma Lula" by hundreds of people that are not relatives.

My Mother, who is 82 years old, recently cooked for and fed over 75 people at her home on Memorial Day weekend. I asked her what the big occasion was, and she simply said, *"It's a meet and greet dinner."*

I have witnessed my Mother show unconditional love to the local bum on the street and to the Pastor of the Church. So much of what we learn about love is learned at home. I consider myself to have come from a loving family. Not perfect, but loving. I am one of four children, all officially "adults." I believe if we were asked, each would say that we have been blessed with a loving, godly Mother and it is my honor to pay tribute to my Momma!

THANK YOU Momma for all the love you have shown me as well as the love you have shown to the many people that you hardly knew. You have always shown nothing but love to everyone you meet; and your love is unconditional. You are truly an ANGEL from GOD.

Love Always, Your Son

Donald Ray

Ollie L. Nash
By Bill Nash

Everyone thinks their Mother is the best and I am no different. "Ma" as I called her was the ultimate Mother as far as I was concerned. She is the one who taught me that a man takes care of his family. She taught me a man goes to work each day even when he doesn't really feel like it. She instilled in me the fact that I should take care of my sisters and stand not only behind them and beside them but in some cases in front of them to shield and protect them from whatever and whoever might cause them harm. Fortunately, both of my sisters chose wisely so defending them hasn't been necessary. My Mother, in conjunction with my Father, taught me to stand tall in the face of adversity and to never shy away from anything or anyone who would seek to do harm to me or my family.

I was blessed with a Mother who was strong in mind, body, soul and most importantly, the Lord. My Mother kept us in church throughout my formative years to the extent that I have imparted that to both of my children. I am happy to say my son and daughter know the Lord and believe in the power of prayer. Ma made me go to church until I reached the age where I wanted to go to church on my own and felt a void when I didn't go. She raised me to be a man of conviction, character and compassion and I have tried to follow her instructions. Since her passing, I still find myself wondering how she would feel about my present position in life and if she would approve or more simply, what she would say about my present status.

Ma has been with the Lord for three years now and not one day goes by that I don't think about her or miss her. I am able to go on because I know within my heart that she would "get on me" if I did anything less. I know that I am the man, husband, father, and brother only because of what she instilled in me. When I feel overwhelmed by life and all its challenges, I just remember her voice when I would call her and she would say, *"Hi sweetheart"* when she realized it was me calling and I am somehow able to make it through whatever I am dealing with. I know I'll never stop loving or missing her, and I always hope and pray that I am becoming the kind of man she would be proud of…I love you Ma.

Bill

Mama
By Ramona Banks

Before we know anything about God and about His great love for us, or know anything about our big brother Jesus and His awesome and obedient sacrifice to save us, or know anything about the Holy Spirit, the very character of our Heavenly Father, or know anything about walking in the plans God has for each and everyone of us, there is "Mama." Mama's love is unconditional and she prays for her children without ceasing. Mama's love never gives up even when she sees her children veering off of the path leading to our Heavenly Creator. Mama is a teacher. Mama is a chastiser. Mama is a mentor. Mama is a friend and a confidant. Mama is our first love.

"Mama"

We heard Mama's voice while we were yet still in her womb
Waiting to be birthed into this world couldn't come too soon
Longing to smell her sweet and unique aroma and to feel her soft skin
Connecting with her on the outside seems a familiar place you've been.

There's a bond with Mama that's comforting and soothing
When your eyes meet with hers it's tantalizing and oh, so very moving
Her smile, her hug, her gentle touch puts your mind at rest
As you giggle and wiggle in her warm caress.

As you blossom, tender young shoot that you are
Mama is there to gird you up, 'cause you're not done yet, by far
As you stumble and fall along the way
Mama is there to pick you up and reassure you knowing just what to say
You see Mama seeks the Highest Counsel from above

96

Not wanting to be wise in her own sight, now, you know that's love.

As you seek advice and Mama's wise nourishing
From listening and being obedient all will see the flourishing
Prosperity that comes from respect and obedience
Because Mama carefully trained and taught on that which has credence
Mama taught you the commands of the Lord to keep them in your heart
Praying from His ways that you'll never depart.

Mama taught you to fear the Lord and shun evil watching you grow in belief
Faith in the Lord as you learn you don't belong to the Thief!
As you grow in knowledge, wisdom, love and power
You learn to escape the snare of the fowler
You start walking with the Lord a life no longer filled with upheaval
As you realize your former path was full of confusion and evil.

Mama looks loving upon you through the eyes of the Father
For you are the clay and He is the Potter
Mama knows He's still molding and shaping you to walk in His plans
For you are His child and upon you is His brand.

Mama has been blessing the Lord all along
She knew you were a gift from the Lord and to Him you belong
Mama set the example and blazed the path; laid the foundation
Watching you walk in your calling; wow, look at God's awesome creation!

Thank you Mama!

In Tribute…
By Cynthia Carlisle Fields

Dear Mothers of the Church:

So long ago, you braved the elements walking if necessary to the place designated as the house of worship. It wasn't much to those who had never entered and taken refuge from a week of strife, hard work and uncertainty. For those who had never laid their cares on the old rickety altar, never released children, grandchildren, husbands into the hands of God, right in this building that no one else wanted; you knew, didn't you, that it didn't matter what it looked like, just what it felt like. You woke us and pulled us from warm beds, bathed and dressed us in our best and brought us to this place, this house of worship and we thank you. For this is the place where we watched you and the others conducting business and writing checks to keep the lights on. In this very place, we learned about David, Daniel and that even if we were small we could slay giants! This was the place, small, old and rundown, where we prayed, dropped our pennies in the collection plate, sold chicken dinners and saw first hand how God made our little into a lot. We drank from the sweat of your brow as you labored right here because this is all we had, all we were allowed to have. *"Amazing grace how sweet the sound…"* that was your mantra and it was indeed sweet, each word ringing in my ears, so young and so naive. I'm sorry for all the times I thought I knew it all, that because you had become old and I had become grown, I had the right not to listen and not remember what true love and sacrifice really looked like.

Now as I sit on royal hued velvet cushions and walk on carpeted floors, I am thankful for those Sundays, Mondays and the rest of the week, that you prayed and made me pray. I am thankful for the times you went without so that I could have what I needed. Thank you Mothers, hmm…such a small word for the big price you paid. This moment is for you and yes, I know it's not enough but I also know you didn't ask for it either for your humility magnifies your wisdom that I can only hope to one day inherit.